PRESERVING NEIGHBORHOODS

PRESERVING NEIGHBORHOODS

How Urban Policy and Community Strategy

Shape Baltimore and Brooklyn

AARON PASSELL

Columbia University Press   *New York*

Columbia University Press
Publishers Since 1893
New York   Chichester, West Sussex
cup.columbia.edu

Library of Congress Cataloging-in-Publication Data
Names: Passell, Aaron, author.
Title: Preserving neighborhoods : how urban policy and community
strategy shape Baltimore and Brooklyn / Aaron Passell.
Description: New York : Columbia University Press, [2021] |
Includes bibliographical references and index.
Identifiers: LCCN 2020028797 (print) | LCCN 2020028798 (ebook)
| ISBN 9780231194068 (hardback) | ISBN 9780231194075 (trade
paperback) | ISBN 9780231550635 (ebook)
Subjects: LCSH: City planning—Maryland—Baltimore. |
City planning—New York (State)—New York. |
Historic preservation—Social aspects—Maryland—Baltimore. |
Historic preservation—Social aspects—New York (State)—
New York. | Historic districts—Maryland—Baltimore. |
Historic districts—New York (State)—New York. |
Urban renewal—Maryland—Baltimore. | Urban renewal—
New York (State)—New York. | Baltimore (Md.)—Social
conditions. | Brooklyn (New York, N.Y.)—Social conditions.
Classification: LCC HT168.B35 P38 2021 (print) | LCC HT168.B35
(ebook) | DDC 307.1/2160974723—dc23
LC record available at https://lccn.loc.gov/2020028797
LC ebook record available at https://lccn.loc.gov/2020028798

Printed in the United States of America

Cover images: (top) Design Pics Inc/Alamy Stock Photo;
(bottom) Adobe Stock
Cover design: Lisa Hamm

To Anne and Rob, who set me on this path,

Luca and Matteo, who help me know what's important,

And Tabatha, my partner in all things.

CONTENTS

ACKNOWLEDGMENTS

The support and encouragement I have relied upon while producing this book are extensive. They range from the interest of old friends, to the attention of colleagues, to the belief of editors, to the support and time investment of family. I could not have accomplished it without those thanked here and myriad others, unnamed or overlooked.

The central Brooklyn research that constitutes half of the book began from a conversation with a dear friend of many years, Jesse Hendrich, who introduced me to Gib Veconi and set off the whole process of investigating Prospect Heights, Crown Heights, and Bedford-Stuyvesant. Gib connected me to Suzanne Spellen, Evelyn Tully Costa, and all of my Prospect Heights interviewees. Suzanne facilitated the connection to Morgan Muncey, who got me into Bed-Stuy. Later in the process, Jesse also introduced me to Rob Witherwax, who connected me in turn to Ethel Tyus. An incidental contact with Cara Soh at a conference in Detroit led to Tenzing Chadotsang. Without the willingness of all to make these connections and to take the time to talk to me, I could not have gone forward.

Johns Hopkins and Eric Holcombe exhibited their commitment to historic preservation in Baltimore with the time they gave me. I owe my connection to them to Elizabeth Nix at the University of Baltimore. In different ways, each welcomed me to the city and revealed how much there is to love about it. Eli Pousson, at Baltimore Heritage, was also generous with his time and data. I began the Baltimore research while teaching at and with support from Muhlenberg College, continued it while teaching part-time at Penn, then reengaged with support from Barnard College. Research funding was important, but more important still was the input from colleagues, particularly Mary Rocco who made a critical suggestion about structuring chapter 5 and Kim Johnson who read early chapters. Friendships with Sevin Yildiz and Gergo Baics have also been integral to my experience at Barnard and facilitated the growth of this work.

A long-time mentor, Harvey Molotch, took this project seriously from the start and helped me move it along at various stages, including dismissing various early and misguided titles. As I hope becomes clear from my admiration for their work, Stephanie Ryberg-Webster and Kelly Kinahan made important contributions by being willing to talk to me about the relationship between historic preservation and neighborhood change when they knew much more about it than I did, which they still do. Kait O'Donnell gave the manuscript careful attention, and it is better for it. My students in the Barnard Urban Studies program, particular my seniors who have been researching and writing alongside me, have listened patiently to a great deal about this work in ways that have helped me advance it.

Eric Schwartz at Columbia University Press could not have been more encouraging about this book, approaching me early in its development and seeing it through to this point, always responsive and humorous. Lowell Frye almost outdoes Eric for professionalism and good cheer and has made this process about as smooth as I can imagine.

None of this could have been either undertaken nor accomplished without the support of a few members of my family. Nadia and Amer have made it possible for me pursue my passion for cities and liberal arts college teaching and have heard a great deal about this book over its evolution, challenging me to explain and reflecting thoughtfully upon it. Thank you. Last, but never least, Tabatha has listened, read, edited, nudged, cooked, cared for children, walked the dog, and more, all while producing her own great and important work. I could not have done it without her and wouldn't have wanted to do so.

PRESERVING NEIGHBORHOODS

1

INTRODUCTION

What does historic preservation do? In the most obvious sense, it saves old buildings, returning them to and keeping them in a robust state, similar to when they were first completed and inhabited (although the exact moment being preserved is worth some thought). Preservationists argue, both explicitly and implicitly, that old buildings deserve this kind of treatment, at least some old buildings do, and that preservation is an appropriate use of resources. Preservation also, its critics like to point out, limits how much and how fast the contemporary city can change and develop by limiting what can be demolished or adapted, privileging the "rights" of old buildings over the dynamics of new development. It does all of these things and others too, such as providing employment and affordable housing, in complex combinations depending on its context. Indeed, what preservation does depends substantially on where it is doing it and the particular history and contemporary conditions of that place.

What does historic preservation do to neighborhoods? It might spur a kind of change that leads to the displacement of current residents, what we generally call gentrification. This is what many researchers assume and low-income housing advocates fear: historic designation triggers an increase in property values (precisely why this should happen is neither specified nor clear) that, in turn, leads to increases in rents and property taxes of the kind that force low- and fixed-income residents out of their homes. It might also enable the defense of a successful neighborhood from change, locking in its status relative to others, disincentivizing flight from demographic transition, and guaranteeing that any newcomers understand the local commitment to historicity as it is articulated as a neighborhood priority.

Historic preservation might preserve a community by discouraging speculative development of the kind that drives prices up, thereby maintaining an affordable supply of housing that serves local interests without attracting relatively wealthier newcomers and, perhaps most important, by bringing locals together in the pursuit of designation in a way that confirms their cohesion and redounds to their longer-term benefit. It might also revitalize a neighborhood by directing investment and development into the area through tax incentives, encouraging a "return to the city" among people—particularly White,[1] middle-class people—who have insisted on suburbia until relatively recently.

Again, historic preservation can do all of these things to neighborhoods, and other things too, but we have to ask the right questions to get at these issues rather than assume any of these connections. Also, which of these particular processes play out and how they do so is radically contingent on the context of the city within which they are occurring. Accordingly, the inquiry into what historic preservation does more generally and does to neighborhoods in particular must first answer "where?" and "when?" before it can proceed (although it also needs to attend to "for whom?"). Despite the importance of historic preservation as a contemporary urban phenomenon, it has yet to be adequately explored from an urban sociological perspective sensitive to its complex interrelation with other neighborhood processes.

I propose to do that here by examining in substantial detail and from multiple directions the relationship of historic preservation to neighborhood change in two very different cases: Baltimore and central Brooklyn. Baltimore is a city made up primarily of older buildings whose population has shrunk radically since its peak around 1950. In Baltimore, preservation advocates and city officials have long been asking what preservation *can* do, attempting to use it as a tool for neighborhood stabilization and revitalization, not fearing change but pursuing it. The results of these efforts vary radically from neighborhood to neighborhood, sometimes seeming to offer hope for progressive change and at other times failing to remedy stagnation or consolidating inequality. In central Brooklyn, community activists are trying to mitigate change through preservation, trying to slow it down, but also finding that preservation advocacy can form the basis of a broader community-building effort. The contrast in cases is intended to highlight the wide range of potential relationships between historic designation and neighborhoods. Preservation is not a unitary phenomenon but a radically contingent one, and we must look hard at the mechanisms through which preservation might affect neighborhoods rather than simply fear displacement.

HISTORIC PRESERVATION AND THE BUILT ENVIRONMENT AS SOCIAL PROCESS

The existing built environment of the city is an inevitable fact. Urban life and urban policy must confront the legacy of processes of development that precede them and incorporate that legacy—its meaning and its material—going forward. The historic city endures in the present; it is not just buildings from one era but from many, and it becomes the context for the contemporary city and the foundation of the future city.

The durability of the historic city compounds the conceptual problem of understanding the urban built environment as a social process,[2] and the effort to do so is essential. The contrary treatment of the physical stuff of the city as a passive container for social life denies how the details of the physical city inform, constrain, and enable the collective life lived within it, obscuring the contributions that past political, economic, and cultural processes continue to make to contemporary life through the structures they have left us. The social life of cities is lived *in interaction* with their physical form. Accordingly, we need to temper the instinctive friction of treating the physical and seemingly static as elements of social process with the knowledge that we confront physical elements from many different moments simultaneously.

The endurance of the historic city, given basic maintenance (which is often too much to presume), is the default. Unless and until someone tears old stuff down, it stands there, serving changing purposes as the city around it changes. There are good reasons to actively preserve the historic city, from the aesthetic concerns most frequently identified with the historic preservation movement to neighborhood-level economic diversity and dynamism as notably described by Jane Jacobs.[3] Actively preserving buildings means making a political and cultural commitment to identifying their "original" state, sometimes obscuring socially productive purposes to which they have been put at other times. This is political, too, in the sense that it draws implicit connections among the structure, its architectural merit, and the politics of the moment from which it emerged, usually regressive politics by current standards. It also opens the common question about the connections between and priorities implicit in the decisions to preserve buildings as opposed to dedicating resources to the people who inhabit them—keeping communities in place.

For the most part, in everyday life our relationship with the past (as with the built environment, more generally) goes unexamined. Historic preservation, the process of regulating the historic built environment to save it, is not so much a departure from common practice as it is the articulation or exaggeration of our typical relationship to old buildings, making explicit a commitment to their continued existence in their historic form. This commitment to historic preservation has been institutionalized at various scales and in varying capacities and has grown into a critical tool for intervening in and managing cities.

As a set of regulations—formal constraints on choice and action—historic preservation policy at the local level draws the ire of the "property rights" crowd,[4] including some prominent scholarly critics perhaps more properly called the "development rights" crowd.[5] They believe preservation impinges on property owners' ability to do what they will with their building, interferes with development, and raises prices in hot housing markets such as New York City. At the same time, the recognition or institutionalization of preservation often does not go far enough for the historically minded, leaving "significant" buildings unprotected and inadequately slowing the march of insensitive new construction. This tension between the champions of the new and the old, along with the difficulty of defining the *when* of historic preservation and the radical variation among American cities in historic trajectories of construction and redevelopment, makes it difficult to know just what historic preservation is in the contemporary city.

It is easy for me, then, to begin by saying that historic preservation *is not one thing*. State and local laws vary in what they protect and how they do it, preservation commissions and non-governmental advocates vary in their orientation and approach, and, most important, American cities are tremendously inconsistent in when they were built up and how much old stuff has survived previous waves of redevelopment (and this, of course, addresses only the U.S. context). It is worth stating that preservation is not one thing because it is often treated as such by its opponents and even by its supporters.

In Boston, Washington, and San Francisco, preservation appears to have enhanced the status of relatively higher-status neighborhoods, producing an effect I think of as "fortification," a term to which preservation advocates generally react poorly. At the same time, and this is better supported, throughout the Rustbelt, city boosters are drawing on preservation as a tool for urban revitalization—or at least stabilization.[6] Again, residents of many cities see designation as a tool for restraining development when it might displace them or, in others, when it is simply displeasing.

If historic preservation is not one thing, it needs to be understood for the things it is, which include being one of the few remaining regulatory mechanisms for affirmatively intervening in the form of the built environment. Whereas land-use zoning generally limits what can be built near what or how elements of the city relate to one another (that is, proscriptive and focused on use rather than form), preservation argues that designated parts of the city *should* look like this, should take this particular shape, and should incorporate these particular details. Preservation regulations are prescriptive in practice and attentive to style. Furthermore, although institutionalized in city and state bureaucracies, much of the work of preservation—from nominations for designation to monitoring and implementation—is done by neighborhood residents, concerned citizens, and other immediately interested parties. This is the reason preservation works both as a tool of revitalization and potentially as one of exclusion.

Stephanie Ryberg-Webster and Kelly L. Kinahan provide us with comparative data about the influence of federal tax credits for historic preservation on shrinking cities that are suggestive of the significance of preservation policy in the current era. I would argue, as I will later in this book, that these data radically underestimate the financial profile of preservation because they do not include local expenditures. In Baltimore, for example, tax incentives have spurred an alleged $1.5 billion in investment.[7] It is difficult to guess the value of Baltimore's expenditures (ten years

TABLE 1.1 COMPARISON OF FEDERAL EXPENDITURE ON RTC, LIHTC, AND CDBG (IN MILLIONS), IN 2010 DOLLARS

	RTC (2000–2010)[1]	LIHTC (2000–2010)[2]	CDBG (2003–2013)[3]
Baltimore	119.9	19.7	275.2
Cleveland	47.2	31.0	284.6
Philadelphia	104.9	57.9	609.2
Providence	43.7	14.9	67.3
Richmond	152.0	7.5	58.7
St. Louis	183.2	16.1	239.7

1 These figures reflect 20 percent of the total RTC investment listed in Table 2, as the RTC is a 20 percent income tax credit on total rehabilitation expenditures. *Source*: National Park Service, Technical Preservation Services.

2 Low Income Housing Tax Credit (LIHTC) projects that do not have an allocation amount in the HUD LIHTC database are excluded from the totals listed here. These figures include LIHTC projects in each city's downtown and its neighborhoods. *Source*: http://lihtc.huduser.org.

3 Data on Community Development Block Grant (CDBG) investments were only available from 2003. Thus we use the ten-year period, 2003–2013, for comparison. CDBG funds are allocated to the city, thus these figures include CDBG money spent in each city's downtown and its neighborhoods. *Source*: https://www.hudexchange.info/grantees/cpd-allocations-awards/.

of foregone tax revenue) on the difference between the original value of historic properties and their value after rehabilitation, but it must be substantial.

Ryberg-Webster and Kinahan show that Community Development Block Grants remain the largest stream of federal expenditure on urban development and redevelopment overall, but the Rehabilitation Tax Credit is the next largest, often much greater than the Low Income Housing Tax Credit.[8] And, as I note, this understates the public investment in historic preservation because many cities and states have important historic tax credit programs.

More important, however, than the details of preservation regulation is the *context* of preservation: preservation is not one thing primarily because it manifests differently in different places. Regulations vary from city to city and state to state, but they have in common the recognition of historic "significance" (some combination of design and historic events or populations) and, often, some protections for historic properties.[9] How these common regulatory commitments play out varies radically according to the age of the city, its demographic composition (and racial history), its redevelopment history, the strength (or weakness) of the real estate market, and who is involved in the preservation process, among other things.

Preservation is not one thing because people put designation to work for very different purposes in cities like Brooklyn and Baltimore. In growing cities with hot markets, historic preservation can moderate the sometimes too rapid pace of redevelopment and can save structures that provide housing at relatively low cost, as well as maintain the distinctive character of neighborhoods and the city as a whole. In shrinking cities or "legacy cities," historic preservation can save the assets that might make an older city appealing going forward, for example, walkable density at the urban core, aesthetically valuable historic structures, and available residential, commercial, and industrial spaces. Our task, then, is to observe preservation in practice and analyze its impact in contrasting contexts.

Our task is also to problematize an assumption operating in both the scholar/activist and neighborhood-resident communities—that historic designation causes gentrification. This is a plausible assumption that scholarship in planning and real estate economics builds upon and that neighborhood activists, particularly in communities of color, respond to, but it has no consistent basis in empirical fact. There are undoubtedly cases in which designation should be connected to price increases and the displacement of longtime residents. In many other cases, however, so many diverse factors are at work that, without even questioning the overstuffed conception of neighborhood change, we can say that the two are not causally related in any automatic sense.

BACKGROUND: FORMALIZING PRESERVATION AND PRESERVATION ORGANIZATIONS

The National Historic Preservation Act was passed in 1966. This law was championed and framed by the United States Conference of Mayors and the National Trust for Historic Preservation (itself founded in 1949) to provide tools to manage the modernization of cities, in general, and urban renewal, in particular.[10] The National Historic Preservation Act established the National Register of Historic Places. Being listed on the National Register protects properties from changes that are funded or initiated by the federal government but does little else beyond the reputational. At the same time, *eligibility* for listing on the National Register is frequently the standard for protection under state and local ordinances. The federal legislation also enabled state historic preservation organizations (SHPOs) and local preservation commissions to make their own regulations appropriate to their jurisdictions. Historic preservation regulation at every level includes the designation of historic landmarks and of historic districts.

What is a historic district (HD)? The answer is quite complicated. Areas can be designated as historic and thereby preserved through legislation at the federal, state, and local levels, with local designation offering the greatest level of protection from significant alteration and the most significant tax incentives.[11]

The National Register defines a *district* in the following way:

> A geographically definable area, urban or rural, possessing a significant concentration, linkage, or continuity of sites, buildings, structures, or objects united by past events or aesthetically by plan or physical development. A district may also comprise individual elements separated geographically but linked by association or history.[12]

HDs comprise "contributing" structures—those that embody the historic significance the district is intended to preserve—and sometimes noncontributing structures that may not be protected under the district definition.

Federal legislation makes possible tax deductions for the additional maintenance costs associated with income-producing historic properties, but it does not have much relevance for residential properties (the exception being historic rental apartment buildings). The benefits that accrue to residential properties located within historic districts are associated primarily with diverse local ordinances. According to the National Trust for Historic Preservation,

> local historic districts are areas in which historic buildings and their settings are protected by public review, and encompass buildings deemed significant to the city's cultural fabric. A property included in a historic district, valued for its historical associations or architectural quality, is worth protecting because it is a virtue to the special and unique personality of the city.[13]

This description does not include the range of potential tax incentives that can accompany local designation, mostly deductions against income for maintenance costs, although sometimes only costs over and above what the maintenance of a nonhistoric property would require are covered.

In addition to tax incentives, local ordinances frequently provide strong protections for historic properties. In New York City, for example, once an individual landmark or contributing building within a landmark district has been *scheduled* for consideration by the citywide Landmarks Preservation Commission (LPC), it cannot be destroyed or significantly altered without the LPC's permission.

The designation of a historic landmark or district constitutes governmental recognition of and support for the claim that elements of the built environment of the city should not change because of their "significance." The meaning of "historical significance" is complex. Historic preservationists' earliest efforts in the United States saved buildings that were symbols of national history and spaces associated with privilege—Jefferson's Monticello, for example. Preservation legislation was pursued in response to the loss of a number of such spaces in the face of ongoing urban modernization (most famously New York City's

Pennsylvania Station). Contemporary preservationists conceive
of themselves as keeping aspects of our material history intact,
up to the scale of neighborhoods, with a sense of significance
that derives from the role of the built environment in historical
moments of social life. Some also believe we can preserve the
"communities" that inhabit these urban spaces; that is, that community is significant and intertwined with place.

Historic preservation organizations in the United States have
recently articulated a broader view of significance, one that recognizes the contributions of people of color, the working class,
immigrants, slaves, and other marginalized or underrepresented
groups in American history (beginning to answer the question
"for whom?"). This means that landmark status is being extended
to spaces that reflect the experience of those Americans, from
ghettos, to tenements, to slave quarters, to the Stonewall Tavern.
The Philadelphia preservationist Patrick Hauck told me that
people still often think of the preservation movement as emphasizing "places where George Washington slept . . . whereas it's
really much broader . . . it's the idea of looking at what's going
on in . . . different neighborhoods where their stories are more
mundane, but they are still the stories of this city."[14]

Preservation's seemingly enduring elitist reputation, particularly among previously underserved populations, may be
changing as urban residents discover the potential of landmarking as a tool for managing development and neighborhood
change. Another Philadelphia preservationist, Melissa Jest,
herself Black, explained the need for people of color to champion preservation to communities of color, but she also warned
that the movement itself, still predominantly White, needed
significant education to grasp that many disadvantaged communities were confronting systemic problems that made preservation issues seem comparatively insignificant. She offered

the paradoxical example of housing affordability for Blacks in historic neighborhoods:

> But what's also happened in that neighborhood that's deterio-
> rated is African Americans have been able to move in because
> prices have gone down, because the properties have gone down.
> So they've been able to get in on the ground floor because of this
> down-spiraling. [But] preservationists come in and they stop it.
> They stop this deterioration and they try to reverse it. It then has
> this positive effect on the values of the property because [they are]
> no longer boarded up, no longer dilapidated. They now are holding
> onto their value or growing in value. . . . So those African Ameri-
> cans who were able to get in because it was affordable for them,
> albeit deteriorating, now find that it's not affordable. . . . They end
> up having to move out, so there you go: "Preservationists came in,
> OK, yeah, it was raggedy here, but we were able to be here, and
> now that they're here, we can't be here." So that's the logic.[15]

Jest argues that this connection is not simply automatic. There are important benefits to lower-income communities of color that pursue designation, but real obstacles also have to be over-come to convince people of these benefits.

This shift toward involving communities historically under-served by preservation efforts is as much about the practical realities of urban policy as it is about ideals of historical significance—what Simeon Bankoff calls the "preservation ethic"[16]—because preservation regulation often provides a mechanism for local control. But this shift also raises the issue of resources, a topic upon which all of my interviewees agree: There are never enough resources available to support all of the preservation efforts that could be undertaken, thus many organizations focus foremost on capacity building in interested communities and providing technical assistance. This movement is meant to facilitate change, but advocates are not always in a position to implement the changes they would like to see. They must rely on the initiative of neighborhood activists with the time, interest, and resources to pursue designation.

ALTERNATIVE THEORIES OF PRESERVATION

My approach to historic preservation is based in an urban sociology of the built environment. I understand that neighborhoods matter—that they *do* something, to paraphrase Robert Sampson[17]—but that intervening in the built environment of the neighborhood constitutes an intervention in complex, interrelated social processes that reverberate in complex and often divergent ways. Many others have approached historic preservation in other ways, and although I am grounded in my specific perspective, I am also speaking to their work across methodological, disciplinary, and temporal divides.

The body of literature that compelled my sociological approach lies somewhere between real estate economics and planning research.[18] This literature attempts, through methods that have become more sophisticated over the decades, to assess the impact on property prices of historic designation. It emerged in the era immediately following the creation of preservation regulations to reassure the real estate industry that preservation would not damage their interests. However, the questions of gentrification and displacement have been evaluated using property prices as a proxy for displacement pressures. This research has produced diverse results, generally implying a positive relationship between designation and price, mostly not in major urban markets, but it is unsatisfying in two primary respects.

First, little of it can specify the causal direction of the relationship (designation producing appreciation or vice versa); second, and more important to me, price appreciation is a poor proxy for the complex relationship between the historic built environment and neighborhood social life. Even in the context of price appreciation, we still need to specify the complex mechanisms through which gentrification produces changes in a neighborhood.

Much of the scholarship on preservation is critical of preservation as a practice.[19] Many planners seem to presume the designation-gentrification-displacement sequence, but it is legal academics and urban economists who are most detailed in their attacks from two very different perspectives. Most legal scholars who take up normative questions around preservation see it as a social justice issue in historic neighborhoods of color, perceiving the designation process as subverting community control and designation itself as exclusion. Urban economists, in contrast, most notably Edward Glaeser, argue that preservation constrains development and compounds affordability issues in hot markets.

I write in reaction to oversimplifying tendencies in various areas of scholarship on historic preservation, but other streams of thought have been more affirmatively influential. There are rare but rigorous studies showing how preservation can contribute to consolidating change in neighborhoods, often following from gentrification-like processes.[20] There is also significant recent scholarship on the role of preservation in revitalizing older cities, legacy cities in particular.[21] These studies helped inform my questions and confirm my case selection.

WHAT LIES AHEAD

In the following chapters, I analyze how preservation efforts have played out in two very different places: Baltimore, Maryland,

and central Brooklyn, New York. In chapter 2, I explore the assumed relationship between preservation and gentrification in Baltimore. I examine demographic change over time in Baltimore historic districts using a number of conventional measures of social status: percent White in a segregated and increasingly majority Black city, college education to capture class and cultural capital, and median household income. Decennial, neighborhood-level data from 1970 to 2010, paired with historic districts and their designation dates, enable me to characterize neighborhood trajectories both before and after designation and to compare them with parts of the city that have never been designated. I also have neighborhood-level data on the Baltimore Historic Tax Credit. I use basic comparisons across designation status, cluster comparisons by designation date, correlation analysis across a range of variables, and matched-pair comparisons in which I track the trajectories of neighborhoods that are similar at baseline: some designated historic, some not.

My conclusion is that Baltimore historic districts are demographically different from never-designated parts of the city and become more different over time. In the few districts that were designated before my data begin, it appears that high-status neighborhoods succeeded in locking in their relative status through designation, which suggests that competence in dealing with city government is important here, what I think of as "institutional capital." In working-class White neighborhoods, historic designation seems to facilitate the in-movement of more educated, higher-paid Whites (displacement is not apparent but would be difficult to observe, given the nature of the data). Historic designation in Baltimore appears to have served distinct purposes in the early period as well as more recently when it incentivizes development through tax credits, although those credits show no predictable pattern of distribution. Finally, across the decades for which I have data, vacancy rates are much higher in historic neighborhoods and often get higher even as the neighborhoods otherwise increase in most status measures.

I complement this quantitative approach to Baltimore neighborhoods with wide-ranging interviews with key players in preservation organizations in Baltimore. This approach enables me to flesh out the overall view of the effects of designation with details and perspectives from the ground.

In chapter 3, my portrait of central Brooklyn draws on recent research on the housing market, crime rates, and neighborhood change, illustrating contrasts with Baltimore. Baltimore is a prominent example of a legacy city, a former manufacturing center that lost significant population in the latter half of the twentieth century, whereas Brooklyn is a substantial and dynamic city of its own and part of a leading global city, perhaps the most important in the world. Brooklyn's real estate markets function differently from those in Baltimore, responding to very different kinds of pressures, although they share a history of White flight, redlining, and deindustrialization.

Preservation advocates in Prospect Heights, Crown Heights, and Bedford-Stuyvesant report pursuing historic or landmark district designation in response to their perception of rapid gentrification in their neighborhoods. I have interviewed a number of these advocates, observed the ad hoc Landmarks Committee of Community Board 3 (in Bed-Stuy), and coded published oral histories of preservationists who were not available to be interviewed. My interviewees range from multigenerational residents, to people who moved into the neighborhood twenty years ago, to those more recently priced out of Manhattan. All of them are cognizant of the rapidly increasing real estate prices in their neighborhoods, including the arrival of international capital, and they refer to "preserving the community" from a variety of perspectives.

These various sources reveal a consistent account of efforts to mitigate change. I place these efforts in their institutional context, describing the ecosystem of preservation organizations in New York City through interviews with current and former staff at the Landmarks Preservation Commission and the Historic Districts Council. Moreover, I examine how organizing around neighborhood preservation issues functions as a community-building exercise.

Recent reports on neighborhood demographics in New York City enable me to confirm the central Brooklyn advocates' sense of change and threat. Data, primarily from the NYU Furman Center,[22] reveal precisely what we refer to as gentrification in central Brooklyn: increasing White population, increasing average educational attainment, increasing household income, and declining housing affordability. Together, however, they do not support the standard view that historic preservation causes gentrification. Here designation clearly follows neighborhood change. Once again, Brooklyn's experience confirms that historic district designation interacts with a range of neighborhood change processes in ways that are contingent on neighborhood history, demography, geography, and institutional capacity.

In chapter 4, I examine how historic preservation interacts with urban processes distinct to legacy cities. Baltimore's physical infrastructure, like that of others, was built to accommodate many more people than the city currently supports. The city now confronts extensive vacancy and abandonment and the problem of how to manage it. Large-scale demolition has recently emerged as the answer to myriad negative impacts abandoned buildings have on neighborhoods, but we need to understand how vacancy interacts with designation and other change factors that I have examined in more detail in earlier chapters.

Housing vacancy stands out as one of the primary ways Baltimore's historic districts differ from other parts of the city.

Vacancy is often much higher in historic districts, even relatively successful ones, both before and after designation. I analyze vacancy and its relationship to preservation and change
in Baltimore neighborhoods. This analysis is important, first,
because of evidence of "demolition by neglect" in historic districts—actively ignored maintenance of vacant buildings leading
to their collapse and opening opportunities for redevelopment
that never would have been permitted otherwise. Second, Baltimore has recently initiated Project CORE (Creating Opportunities for Renewal and Enterprise), a large-scale, abandoned
housing demolition program similar to those in other legacy
cities, intended to remove four thousand houses over five years.
Much of that housing is in historic neighborhoods, and Project
CORE will affect the trajectory of those neighborhoods and the
meaning of district designation in Baltimore going forward. I
also draw on archival documents to unpack residents' sense of
demolition by neglect.

In chapter 5, I further explore the ways in which organizing
around neighborhood preservation issues functions as a community-building exercise, examining the activities of central
Brooklyn preservation advocates as they *enforce* landmark district regulations and struggle to create new districts. I observed
the ad hoc landmarks committee of Community Board 3 in
Bedford-Stuyvesant and interviewed leaders of the Landmarks
Committee of the Prospect Heights Neighborhood Development Council and Community Board 8 to understand how local
volunteers respond to varying efforts to alter historic buildings
within landmark districts. I look at who chooses to engage in
these enforcement efforts, how they talk about their neighbors
and neighborhoods, and how they manage development. Finally,
I recount the struggle to create a Crown Heights South district
and the process of designating or developing a landmark in the
neighborhood, the Bedford Union Armory. These struggles

point to the kinds of obstacles advocates still confront in preserving places.

In chapter 6, I return to the findings of my Baltimore and Brooklyn research, putting the role of preservation in each of these cities into contrast with the positions on preservation most common in the literature. I highlight the different purposes to which preservation regulation can be put, different from those for which it was designed, but I also point to the particularity of the city itself and how that shapes the choices neighborhood activists, professional advocates, and city officials make in regard to pursuing preservation. For example, the recent history of rapid neighborhood change in central Brooklyn brings into focus how the work of landmarking there is part of a community-building effort to fight displacement.

Baltimore and central Brooklyn are not precisely opposite ends of a spectrum of urban trajectories, but they do represent radically different urban contexts that reveal differences in how preservation efforts can manifest. The most distinct contrast is obviously between facilitating revitalization in Baltimore and mitigating gentrification in Brooklyn. Given the federal government's relative withdrawal from urban policy since the 1980s, I argue that the application of preservation regulations and the incentives that come with them in some cities and states are the primary policy tools that provide local actors with any control over the built environment. The questions that emerge from the research encompassed here point to future research in cities elsewhere on the development spectrum, for example, Philadelphia, which has the qualities of both a legacy city and a rapidly growing one. They also raise questions about how urbanists *should* understand preservation, and I weigh in on this question.

2

EXPLAINING CHANGE IN BALTIMORE'S HISTORIC NEIGHBORHOODS

I n this chapter, I begin to unpack the complex, contingent, and contextual relationship between historic preservation and neighborhood change in Baltimore, a well-known legacy city. A legacy city has declined from historic heights of population, industry, and employment but has enduring built resources— the *legacy* of historic conditions. Baltimore falls near one end of a spectrum of American cities, with plentiful (even redundant) historic resources, whereas Brooklyn (see chapter 3) is at the other end of the spectrum, competition for space is fierce and development and affordability issues are common. Another contrast is that preservation efforts in Baltimore are substantially top-down, or initiated by government, at least more recently, whereas those in central Brooklyn are much more bottom-up, initiated by local residents.

Much of the literature on historic preservation assumes that historic district designation causes gentrification. The designation-gentrification story is not an implausible one: historic district designation could recognize and lock in home value, which then appreciates, increasing property taxes and encouraging longtime homeowners to sell to wealthy newcomers, raising rents, and displacing renters. Some evidence of property value increases does exist, although this is contested.[1] But evidence of the causal chain running in the opposite direction is also seen; that is, designation following gentrification. As far back as the mid-1980s, sociologist Philip Kasinitz identified a kind of "pull up the ladder behind you" phenomenon in Boerum Hill, Brooklyn, which gentrified in a pretty classic fashion, then consolidated the investments of newcomers by renaming (or branding) itself and landmarking, distinguishing itself from its working-class recent past and limiting future changes to those in line with the new vision for the neighborhood.[2]

I have two causal chains to test—designation then gentrification and vice versa—but I also have to take seriously the possibility that this relationship is not causal, which would explain the difficulty past scholars have had in demonstrating it. Designation and gentrification could be two among many complex urban processes only distantly related to one another, each one more intensely connected to other urban phenomena. Moreover, even if there is a causal relationship in some instances, the presumption that it is uniform across neighborhoods and cities could easily be false. American cities are often as different from one another as they are similar, and so are neighborhoods.

My research on historic preservation and neighborhood change in Baltimore is consistent with more recent scholarship investigating the relationship,[3] and it strongly confirms that the association between historic preservation and neighborhood change is significantly more complex than previously understood. Furthermore, because this relationship is contingent on the particular history and political economy of each neighborhood, nested in a city of interrelated neighborhoods, it does not even play out uniformly across different neighborhoods within a single city.

Three trends in my data on Baltimore neighborhoods, in particular, complicate the dominant narrative in the literature. First, neighborhoods of substantially higher status (Whiter and more educated) in the late 1960s and early 1970s that designated as historic districts were more likely to maintain or amplify that higher status relative to never-designated neighborhoods, at least in terms of income and education. This is not gentrification as we usually understand it; these were longtime, high status neighborhoods that locked in their relative prestige through historic designation, a kind of "fortification." I find historic designation associated with the consolidation of an upper-middle-class Black neighborhood similar in some respects (see Original Northwood later in the chapter), but it is again not a typical gentrification story.

Second, my data show that working-class White neighborhoods in Baltimore that designate as historic districts are closest to the conventional story. Radical increases in educational attainment and income often follow designation in these neighborhoods, in both absolute terms and relative to never-designated neighborhoods. In comparison, working-class black neighborhoods that designate show no such association, pointing to a demographic aspect of the contingency of the relationship. Although displacement fears are focused on and among neighborhoods of color, working class White neighborhoods are often first to change, which fits with my general sense from the gentrification literature.

Finally, my research indicates that we must attend more carefully to other urban phenomena if we are to understand the dynamics of gentrification in any city. In Baltimore, it is impossible to understand either historic preservation or neighborhood investment without acknowledging the influence of the Baltimore Historic Tax Credit (HTC) Program. Significant investments have taken place in historic neighborhoods all over the city in response to the credit. Variations in how the HTC is distributed and how it channels investment point to how the intricate and entangled complex geography of Baltimore affects differences in institutional capacity and the density of the remaining urban fabric.

I begin with interview data positioning the preservation process and the city's ambitions for it, letting the major players in Baltimore preservation frame the analysis. Then I report on the numerically observable differences between designated historic districts and never-designated neighborhoods in general and how they change over time. I return to interview data on the historical and more recent role of preservation efforts in Baltimore, and then return to a detailed examination of quantitative data on the clusters of historic districts that share designation dates in common in comparison to the rest of the city. I unpack Baltimore's HTC and analyze its distribution; then I consider insights revealed by correlation analysis and matching historic districts with never-designated neighborhoods like them, when I chart their respective trajectories.

PRESERVATION AND NEIGHBORHOOD CHANGE IN BALTIMORE

Historic preservation has been central to Baltimore's recent ambitions. Like many American cities, and legacy cities in particular, Baltimore began losing population in the 1950s when jobs and working- and middle-class Whites left the city. Former city residents moved to the suburbs in the post-WWII housing boom, and manufacturing jobs moved to the suburbs, the South, and eventually abroad. The city's population reached nearly one million in 1950 but has declined steadily since then (although flattening briefly between 2011 and 2014). By 2017, the population of Baltimore was 611,648, a 35.6 percent drop since 1950.[4]

As noted previously, the city's long history, combined with this decline in population, has left Baltimore with the dubious resource of an extensive and underused historic built environment. Capitalizing on that resource has involved aggressive adoption of historic preservation regulations to forestall American urban development history's tendency toward demolition (although Baltimore is an exporter of "antique" bricks). One beginning of this story of adopting preservation regulation is in the so-called highway wars of the late 1960s and early 1970s over the location of Interstate 95. The leading plan for the route of the highway took it through Fells Point and Canton, threatening destruction of what are now two of the more successful city neighborhoods.[5] The local fight against that route relied on the newly available, at the time, mechanism of National Register of Historic Places designation, which protected designated districts from demolition funded by federal programs. Fells Point was one of the earliest districts to designate (1969), and it has become an important tourist destination. Canton designated later (1980), but it has since been transformed by gentrification.

Baltimore Heritage and the Baltimore Commission for Historic and Architectural Preservation, founded in 1960 and 1964, respectively, were already in place at the time of the struggle over I-95. These organizations and their advocacy for historic neighborhoods would grow in importance over the years, as the city struggled to manage population decline and sought revitalization through policies such as the Baltimore City Tax Credit for Historic Rehabilitations and Restorations, beginning in 1996. Major anchor institutions, including Johns Hopkins University, also contributed to these efforts as have newer employers such as Under Armour. Designated historic districts—both National Register of Historic Places and those locally designated—proliferated from the late 1960s, totaling eighty-six in 2018.

This proliferation is not responsible for, but is related to, the revi-talization and redevelopment of a number of Baltimore neighbor-hoods, producing a curious geography that mixes gentrification and decline in a patchwork across a city that continues to shrink.

Eric Holcomb,[6] director of Baltimore's Commission for Historic and Architectural Preservation (CHAP), describes an increasing acceptance of a pro-preservation position in Balti-more. By 2016, he felt that people had become generally ame-nable to designation. The CHAP oversight that comes with local designation used to be "a hard sell," Holcomb observed, but homebuyers and homeowners are increasingly familiar with similar kinds of constraints imposed by homeowners' associa-tions and are no longer so easily deterred. Homeowners' asso-ciations, common in recent suburban subdivisions, often control the appearance of houses in significant detail and exercise veto power over proposed changes.[7]

Notably, Holcomb reported, local designation in low-income neighborhoods is increasing. He explained that longtime CHAP director Kathleen Kotarba understood and established district designation in Baltimore as a source of local control for neighborhoods over their built environment, particularly given the history of urban renewal. As noted elsewhere, much of Bal-timore's built environment is historic, and recently designated neighborhoods are increasingly like the rest of the city.

A number of factors reinforce the pro-preservation tendency that Holcomb identifies. He reported a "shrinking" designation process at the local level. From the mid-1960s to the late 1980s, signs were posted in neighborhoods to alert residents of an impending district designation determination. Multiple hear-ings were followed by the consideration and passage of a city council ordinance (for each district). That shifted in the 1990s to a petition requesting designation signed by a significant or "healthy" majority of affected homeowners (with no precise definition of that majority specified, implying some room for interpretation). That process gave way, in turn, to a mailing to homeowners in the proposed district with a support/oppose card to return, followed by a hearing. The process now involves a letter to homeowners and an online survey. This shrinkage, or streamlining, of the process makes community comment possible but is less likely to encourage resistance because it removes those aspects of the public process most likely to facilitate organization—public meetings.

Second, in Baltimore, there has been consequential financial support for demonstrating historical "significance," a necessary first step in designation and a complicated process that frequently requires a professional preservationist. Support for designation has come either from a grant program run by Preservation Maryland (which may no longer be funding this particular activity but certainly did so through the early 2000s)[8] or from mitigation arrangements—compensation from developers for being allowed to demolish something historic elsewhere. Obviously, both of these forms of support facilitate designation independent of the resources of a neighborhood's residents.

Third, the city provides a property tax credit (the HTC) for rehabilitating any contributing structure in a historic district. The credit protects developers and homeowners who invest in historic properties from the tax consequences of improving the value of a structure for ten years, and it is transferable. According to Holcomb, small developers in East Baltimore frequently use the credit to refurbish row houses for sale to relatively higher-status in-movers, which may have hastened the radical change in the neighborhood, or gentrification, over the past twenty years.

Holcomb described a context in which preservation has been taken up as a tool by policy makers, incentivized through tax relief and support for designation, and has facilitated and focused investment in historic neighborhoods. This has encouraged movement into the city by young, predominantly White professionals who value historic aesthetics. When asked whether he believes historic preservation might be related to gentrification, Holcomb responded skeptically: "What is gentrification?"

Holcomb's answer to his own question is revealing. He explained that we might think of gentrification in terms as diverse as revitalization, racial change, economic status change, or generational change. Although acknowledging that some of these changes are problematic, Holcomb argued forcefully that revitalization is a good thing for Baltimore and that preservation policies are the single most positive and effective tool for neighborhood revitalization. He emphasized the success of South Baltimore, for example, which is transitioning from working-class White to young professionals, and that reinforces some of my own findings.

Numerical Data on Historic Districts and Neighborhood Change

Baltimore's efforts to encourage historic district designation are demonstrable. CHAP lists eighty-six historic districts that have been designated since 1969, of which fifty-five are predominantly residential neighborhoods significantly coterminous with "neighborhood statistical areas" (NSAs), for which the city provided demographic data from 1980 through 2010. All told, seventy-three NSAs fall primarily within historic districts, which may encompass multiple neighborhoods, and 155 neighborhoods do not significantly overlap with a historic district, enabling a demographic comparison of historic neighborhoods and never-designated parts of the city and change over time.

Has historic preservation in Baltimore led to the neighbor-hood revitalization that many scholars anticipate? My numeri-cal data (discussed here and later in the chapter) show that historic districts in Baltimore[9] are different from the parts of the city that have never been designated. I cannot confirm the causal relationship Holcomb claimed between preservation and revi-talization, but historic district designation is clearly interacting with neighborhood demographics in a profound fashion.

As White flight in Baltimore (beginning in the 1950s) contin-ued into the 1980s and 1990s, historic districts (HDs) lost their White population more slowly, going from somewhat Whiter to much Whiter than the rest of the city, although they still shift from majority White to majority Black over this period (table 2.1). There is slightly less variation among HDs, but large standard deviations indicate a great deal of variation among neighborhoods in the same category (HDs or never-designated neighborhoods).

Residents of Baltimore's HDs are also markedly more edu-cated than those in undesignated neighborhoods, at least more recently. (Measured by percentage with a bachelor's degree or higher.) As educational attainment increased generally in the United States, it increased much faster in Baltimore historic districts, until it is now almost twice the average in never-designated neighborhoods (figure 2.1).

TABLE 2.1 AVERAGE PERCENT WHITE IN HISTORIC VS. NEVER-DESIGNATED NEIGHBORHOODS IN BALTIMORE

	% White 1970	% White 1980	% White 1990	% White 2000	% White 2010
Historic Districts	58.9	58.9	53.1	41.5	41.3
Never-Designated Areas	53.7	46.0	37.7	28.2	24.2

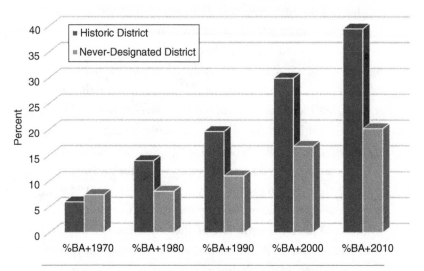

FIGURE 2.1 Comparison of average percent bachelor degree or above (BA+) in neighborhood statistical area by designation status

Finally, the average median family/household income (MFI/MHI) in HDs increases steadily as a proportion of the average MFI/MHI in never-designated neighborhoods, ranging from 92.2 percent in 1970 to 130.9 percent in 2010, meaning that historic districts start slightly poorer and wind up substantially higher earning, on average (figure 2.2).

In summary, despite the high variability among neighborhoods of both types, Baltimore HDs appear different from never-designated neighborhoods in that the population in HDs have achieved higher status, at least to the degree that Whiteness, advanced educational attainment, and higher median household income serve as plausible indicators of socioeconomic status. Moreover, although I cannot yet explain the variation *within* category (HD vs. never-designated neighborhoods), its very existence points to the contingency and contextuality of particular cases of designation.

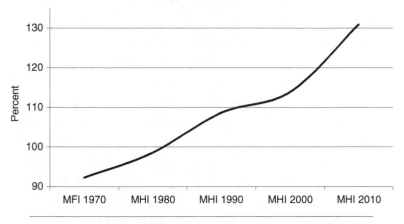

FIGURE 2.2 Median family income (MFI) or median household income (MHI) in historic districts as a percent of never-designated districts

I cannot yet discern causal direction; that is, whether already higher-status neighborhoods were designated or whether designated neighborhoods attracted higher-status in-movers. There are hints, though: forty of the fifty-five (73 percent) HDs for which I have data were designated after 2000, so my first four data points (1970–2000) provide predesignation data. Data on higher-status measures in NSAs that will become HDs suggest that relative status gains often *precede* designation in Baltimore. That HDs appear different (divergent from never-designated neighborhoods), and increasingly so over time, is interesting regardless.

More on Preservation in Baltimore

Johns Hopkins,[10] executive director of Baltimore Heritage, the city's leading preservation advocacy nonprofit, provided important context and historical background with regard to preservation in Baltimore. Architect Bo Kelly founded Baltimore Heritage in 1960 and helped to establish CHAP in 1964, serving as its first chair. Hopkins characterized Kelly as a historical force unto himself, essential to the trajectory of preservation in the city. Kelly envisioned the two organizations as complementary, according to Hopkins.[11] Baltimore Heritage cannot regulate, but it is not subject to the kind of political pressure CHAP faces from the mayor and city council, so its advocacy for preservation can be more straightforward and concerted. CHAP, in contrast, designates historic landmarks and districts and enforces the regulations pertaining to them, but it functions primarily as a responsive or reactive bureaucracy, not as an advocacy organization.

Notably, and similar to Holcomb, gentrification in Baltimore is not a pressing concern for Hopkins. The revitalization that preservation might bring seems to him to carry little risk: "Many disinvested Baltimore neighborhoods need more economic diversity to be healthy and have plenty of room to grow without displacement."[12] He explained that even the most affluent neighborhoods in the city are bordered by disinvestment—unlike New York City and San Francisco, where displacement can mean being forced to leave the city entirely—so affordable housing options are available *near* every Baltimore neighborhood. If some residents are displaced through gentrification processes, they need not be displaced very far. However, any displacement can critically undermine neighborhood networks upon which people with fewer resources, in particular, depend.[13]

Hopkins further explained that the level of disinvestment in Baltimore has led to Project CORE, a city plan with state funding for the demolition of 4,000–5,000 houses in the city (see chapter 4). He regrets the loss of any historic properties but recognizes that strategic demolitions that are part of a comprehensive plan, rather than arbitrary or ad hoc, might help neighborhoods. At the very least, neighborhood residents have been convinced in Cleveland, Detroit, and Buffalo that demolition can help, and they support local and state efforts to undertake it. Rather than heedlessly defying this trend, Baltimore Heritage has insisted on becoming part of the team identifying locations to focus on for demolition.

Like Holcomb, Hopkins believes that preservation in Baltimore is producing revitalization. He claimed that the hottest neighborhoods in the city are all historic, and in addition, each has some kind of signature building at its center, a redeveloped landmark. For example, Canton has been transformed from a working-class White neighborhood into a neighborhood of highly educated, White professionals, a transformation driven by Baltimore developer Bill Struever's use of the city's historic tax credit to rehabilitate the American Can Company, a large former industrial building at the neighborhood's waterfront edge that is now luxury condos. According to Hopkins, Struever pulled off a similar effect in Locust Point, rehabilitating a former Procter and Gamble factory into "funky" offices, which the Under Armour corporation then made their headquarters. On a smaller scale and more recently, Remington is undergoing a "revitalization sparked by thirty-something hipsters" that is centered around the adaptive reuse of a historic automotive showroom.

Finally, Hopkins drew my attention to the technical and economic implications of different types of historic district designation. He emphasized the distinction between National Register of Historic Places (NRHP) designation, overseen by the National Park Service, and local designation, administered by the city of Baltimore. NRHP designation establishes eligibility for tax credits from the city and state (and for income-producing

properties from the federal government), but NRHP designation has "no strings attached," meaning that it comes with
minimal mechanisms for prohibiting demolition or control-
ling alterations. In Baltimore, most locally designated districts
are also NRHP designated, but the reverse is not true (districts
originally designated by the NRHP do not necessarily also pursue local designation).

The positive side of this noninvasive type of designation is
that it does not require significant cooperation from property
owners and can, in fact, effectively come from above (top-down)
without much community involvement, according to Hopkins
(he also called these "stealth" designations). Baltimore developers will sometimes pay for the services of the professional preservationist required to make a comprehensive argument about a
neighborhood's historic merit for nomination as part of a mitigation agreement, allowing developers to demolish something
that preservation advocates would otherwise fight to save, sometimes in another part of the city. This expense is not insignificant,
and the NRHP designation enables all local property owners of
contributing buildings to access tax credits.

Only local designation provides community control over the
landscape because locally designated districts require CHAP
approvals for alteration and demolition and involve locals in
the process, particularly as the ongoing observers of threats to
historic properties. Accordingly, Hopkins said that the only
way to really protect a neighborhood is through local designation. He further suggested that the pursuit of local designation
is usually triggered by demolition pressure (a trend consistent
with the experiences of central Brooklyn explored in chapter 3)
or changes to the physical fabric of the neighborhood. Hopkins sees a wave of local designation going on right now, but he
complains that there is not enough city staff to manage all of it.

This complicates my top-down account of Baltimore. Although NRHP designation often occurs in a top-down fashion, local register designation is more likely to begin with community efforts, thus bottom-up.

Designation Clusters

The contemporary wave of designations that Hopkins sees would not be the first. Examining the NRHP designation dates of Baltimore historic districts reveals four temporal clusters of HDs, three of them quite tight, the fourth a little looser. Six districts were designated between 1969 and 1974, eight between 1980 and 1983, one in 1987, one in 1998, twenty-two between 2001 and 2004, and seventeen between 2006 and 2015 (the loosest cluster).

This clustering raises significant questions about the political forces at work as well as numerous other factors that play into the question of why a neighborhood designates when it does (or fails to) and points to the need for further qualitative investigation. For now, though, the existence of distinct waves offers an opportunity to explore measurable differences among these clusters and the degree to which they reveal different relationships between designation and neighborhood social status.

The earliest and most distinctive cluster, 1969 to 1974 (six HDs), includes districts designated in the first decade during which designation became a legal possibility. These neighborhoods are Bolton Hill, Dickeyville, Federal Hill, Fells Point, Mount Vernon, and Roland Park. As one might imagine, these six neighborhoods are the most conspicuously historic in the city, essentially a backlog of widely treasured places at the time of their designation. They include dignified three-story brick row houses on tree-lined boulevards and quaint, cobblestone market squares on the waterfront. These neighborhoods also must have included residents attuned to the availability of historic designation (early adopters) and its potential benefits (mostly just recognition or reputation until 1996) and people who were culturally, politically, and economically capable of navigating the designation process.

It is perhaps not surprising, then, that this cluster had the highest status population of the bunch prior to designation, or that the difference in status has been further amplified over the following decades. In 1970, HDs designated between 1969 and 1973 are two-thirds more White than never-designated parts of the city, reaching twice as White by some time between 1980 and 1990, and three times as White by 2010. Both the cluster and never-designated neighborhoods decline in Whiteness in absolute terms over this period: from 90 percent to 75 percent for HDs and 54 percent to 24 percent for never-designated neighborhoods. Standard deviations in the cluster average are smaller in this early cluster than in the others, meaning that HDs within this cluster are more like each other.

These early HDs contained almost two-and-a-half times as many residents with a BA as never-designated neighborhoods did in 1970. Once again, this increases to nearly four times as many in 1980 and 1990, settling back to approximately three times as many in 2000 and 2010. The percentages themselves are more telling: never-designated neighborhoods increase steadily from 7.3 percent BA+ in 1970 to 24.2 percent BA+ in 2010 (well below the national average of 32 percent), whereas HDs increase from 17.4 percent in 1970 to 70 percent in 2010 (figure 2.3). Putting this difference in perspective, this means that within these six HDs Baltimore—a failing city by many measures—looks like the elite areas of other American cities. Kinahan finds a similar pattern in St. Louis in respect to a

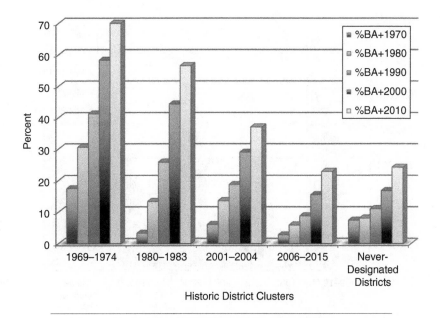

FIGURE 2.3 Educational attainment in historic district clusters and never-designated districts, 1970–2010

neighborhood called Lafayette Square, the first designated in that city (in the early 1970s).[14]

The median income (MFI/MHI[15]) in these HDs is slightly greater than the never-designated neighborhoods average in 1970 ($9,877 compared to $8,815), but the median income in HDs is almost two-thirds greater (+$26,118) by 2010 (figure 2.4).[16]

Two dynamics seems to be at work in this earliest cluster of HD designations. First, as noted previously, the neighborhoods that designated early were generally higher-status neighborhoods to begin with—Whiter and better educated, although not much higher earners than the average household. These neighborhoods provide the clearest instance of designation following

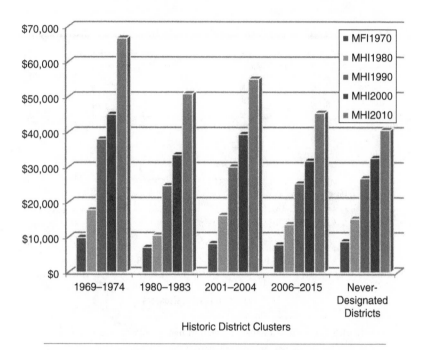

FIGURE 2.4 Income in historic district clusters and never-designated districts, 1970–2010

from status, primarily because the cultural and institutional competency that accompany status were critical to the capability to take advantage of the regulatory opportunity, which, when new, was almost certainly pursued by community actors. What is left unanswered is whether this causal trajectory is limited to this period or pertains more broadly. Second, designation appears to alter the trajectory of these neighborhoods relative to others, slowing change in racial composition while accelerating it with regard to education and income. Status and designation seem to be entangled, neither one simply causing the other nor responding to it.

It is important, however, to recognize the characteristics that are not distinct to this cluster. All of the neighborhoods in all of the clusters of HDs contain more residents with higher levels of education immediately prior to their period of designation, regardless of deeper historical levels. All of the clusters also show more rapidly increasing rates of educational attainment and income than never-designated neighborhoods, both prior to and after designation. The 2006–2015 cluster is most like the never-designated parts of the city, probably because the financial incentives associated with the historic tax credit introduced in 1996 encourage designation of lower-status parts of the city as a way to channel revitalization funding to these areas.

Summing up the distinctions among clusters, the first cluster (1969–1974, six HDs) had the highest status population. White elites were still living in these historic neighborhoods that opted to designate in the early 1970s despite the gathering momentum of White flight. The next cluster (1980–1983, eight HDs) is substantially better educated than never-designated neighborhoods elsewhere in the city, but much poorer than the average Baltimore neighborhood, both before and for twenty years after designation, and in that sense has the lowest status of the clusters. The third cluster (2001–2004, twenty-two HDs) is Whiter and better educated than the rest of the city, but not so distinctly as the earliest cluster, and its income level is average, making it the second highest status of the four. It is also the first cluster in the era of the city's HTC, instituted in 1996 (figure 2.5).

In contrast, the fourth and loosest cluster (2006–2015, seventeen HDs) is average almost across the board, suggesting that whatever status-related connections may have operated in the earlier clusters, they are no longer in operation—designated neighborhoods are now like the average neighborhood, if such a thing exists. If Baltimore's efforts to use historic district designation to trigger

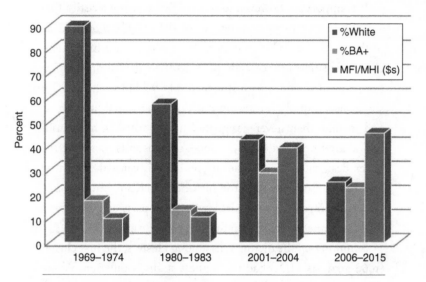

FIGURE 2.5 Cluster characteristics prior to designation

neighborhood revitalization is working, it is in these clusters. The question is whether or not designation is working to revitalize neighborhoods.

A partial answer emerges if I compare each HD cluster to never-designated neighborhoods during a similar time period. Figure 2.6 displays the characteristics of each cluster *relative* to never-designated parts of the city at the baseline observation for that cluster (1970, 1980, 2000, and 2010). I have taken the baseline reading for each cluster and divided it by the average in never-designated parts of the city. Presenting the data this way points to the higher status of the earliest HDs and to the fact that the latest cluster closely resembles the rest of the city prior to designation. This may be an effect of Baltimore's HTC and the effort to use historic designation to incentivize revitalization (top-down as opposed to bottom-up designation): designation

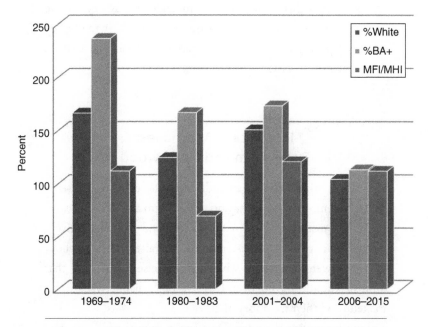

FIGURE 2.6 Historic district cluster neighborhood characteristics relative to never-designated districts prior to designation

happens in lower-status neighborhoods with greater frequency in neighborhoods that are historic but otherwise much like the rest of the city (much of which is historic). In the most recent cluster, income is already higher than that of never-designated neighborhoods by 2010, and these neighborhoods go from being slightly less White to being slightly more White between 2000 and 2010, both suggesting some effect of designation.

This analysis demonstrates that educational attainment *predicts* designation better than income and reveals that HDs are relatively culturally capital-rich neighborhoods that may not command extraordinary economic capital. Income in HDs prior to designation is very close to that in the rest of the city except in the early 1980s cluster, in which it is much lower. However, there are one-and-a-half to two-and-a-quarter times as many highly educated people in neighborhoods about to designate than in other parts of the city.

Interesting Anomalies:
Downtown and Northwood

Historic districts Downtown and Original Northwood deserve special attention because they do not fall into any of the clusters previously discussed. Designated in 1987 and 1998, respectively, neither belongs with a cluster, and both raise questions about why they were designated when nothing else was getting that kind of attention. Moreover, they are both distinctive in their makeup and their trajectory of change.

I am borrowing the name Downtown from the NSA map—this area actually includes three HDs: Cathedral Hill (1987), Business and Government Center (1997), and Market Center (2000). Many of the contributing buildings in the HDs are commercial or institutional rather than residential, but the area still has a residential population close to the NSA average (2,852 in 1980). Cathedral Hill contains most of that residential population, so Downtown's population is roughly synonymous with that of Cathedral Hill.

Downtown may be the strongest candidate for gentrification following designation in Baltimore. The area begins Whiter than any but the 1969–1974 cluster, much Whiter than the rest of the city, but loses White population much the fastest between 1980 and 2000 (table 2.2). The White population of all of the HD clusters stabilized between 2000 and 2010, or even increased slightly, but in Downtown the White population *increased* by 7.4

TABLE 2.2 DOWNTOWN'S DEMOGRAPHIC CHARACTERISTICS

Downtown	% White	% BA+	MFI/MHI
1970	83.1	23.6	$9,727
1980	75.9	16.6	$8,199
1990	56.5	30.0	$19,641
2000	41.2	40.3	$24,657
2010	48.6	80.8	$37,820

percent. Similarly, Downtown begins strictly middle of the pack (of HD clusters) in terms of BA+, but it explodes in the 2000–2010 period to become the most educated of any of the clusters by 10 percentage points. In terms of income, Downtown starts lowest, tracks closely with all of the HD clusters except Original Northwood across the period, and ends lowest.

Finally, it is worth nothing that Downtown's total population declines by about one-third between 1990 and 2000, but it increases almost two-and-a-half times by 2010. It would appear that large numbers of highly educated, low-earning Whites moved into the neighborhood in the 2000 to 2010 period, the classic gentrification story of risk-tolerant artists, musicians, and recent college graduate "pioneers."

Original Northwood also proves to be unique in a number of respects. At the two data points prior to its designation,[17] Original Northwood is slightly Whiter than the average historic district and more than 50 percent Whiter than the average never-designated neighborhood. However, it falls below the 70 percent White mark, which tends to characterize stable integrated neighborhoods—ones that maintain a degree of racial mixing in the perceived safety of a significant White majority.[18] But in the two observations *after* designation, it has become much less

TABLE 2.3 ORIGINAL NORTHWOOD'S DEMOGRAPHIC CHARACTERISTICS

Original Northwood	% White	% BA+	MHI
1980	65.8	28.8	$24,276
1990	59.8	43.4	$53,855
2000	37.9	57.4	$64,688
2010	37.5	65.4	$79,861

White than any of the other HD clusters, although it is still Whiter than the never-designated neighborhoods. Even more curious, racial change seems to stabilize between 2000 and 2010 (table 2.3).

More interesting than the racial demographics is how they combine with the educational attainment and income statistics for the neighborhood. In Baltimore and across the United States, race and education and race and income are significantly and substantially correlated—those more educated and higher paid are most often White rather than Black. Original Northwood defies this relationship. Even as it shifts from majority White to majority Black, it remains roughly as well educated as the highest status cluster of HDs (1969–1974), home to Baltimore's White elite. Original Northwood is, in fact, more educated than any other HD cluster (except Downtown). MHI in Original Northwood is 37 percent greater in 1980 than MHI in the 1969–1974 cluster, otherwise the highest income. It increases faster over the next ten years to 42 percent greater than the 1969–1974 cluster, again otherwise the highest income. The earliest cluster catches up somewhat, but Northwood's MHI in 2010 ($79,861) is still 20 percent greater.

Original Northwood is now a significant African American majority neighborhood that is relatively well-educated and high earning. There is a transition period, 1980 to 1990, in which the neighborhood became significantly more educated and significantly higher earning. It then designated and lost much of its White population without reversing the trends in education or income.

This is not a gentrification-then-designation story because the neighborhood was already relatively high status in 1980. Rather, it is an upper-middle-class, somewhat integrated White neighborhood that became an upper-middle-class, somewhat integrated Black neighborhood.

As much as anything, Northwood points to how many stories are lost in the broader-brush picture I have been trying to paint about historic district designation in Baltimore, even if the aggregate data do tell us something useful. Original Northwood shouts out the same thing that both the large standard deviations and the remaining analysis indicate—preservation is not one thing even in a *single* city.

BALTIMORE HISTORIC TAX CREDIT

It is important to delve deeper into the details of the Baltimore HTC to understand its significance. How is the relationship between historic district designation and neighborhood change affected by factors outside the phenomena themselves? The tax credit tries to channel investment into historic neighborhoods by incentivizing redevelopment there. In some sense, this is an attempt to force the designation-gentrification trajectory, but in the context of Baltimore it extends also to the creation of affordable housing.

In Baltimore, as Holcomb's and Hopkins's comments reveal, historic district designation has been one of an array of policies, including tax incentives for employers and the resale of city-owned residential properties for nominal prices, employed in an effort to foster neighborhood revitalization and economic growth. The HTC has sought to create an economic incentive to seek designation by removing financial disincentives associated with investment in rehabilitation. The use of the tax credit and its geographic distribution are new variables to consider in the relationship between historic preservation and neighborhood change.

The Baltimore HTC is intended to attract investment in underutilized historic structures. Baltimore and other older American cities have a significant asset—a wealth of (potentially) beautiful old buildings. Unfortunately, property tax rules often act as a disincentive to restoring these properties because restored properties incur greater tax liability. Baltimore's HTC is structured to remove the disincentive of increased property taxes associated with changes in value following the significant rehabilitation of a property. Property owners receive a ten-year credit covering the difference in the tax assessed on the postrehabilitation building and its prerehabilitation value. Although the assessed tax increases with the rehabilitation of the property and associated increase in property value, the property owner does not pay that increase for the first ten years after rehabilitation. The credit is available for both residential and commercial properties in which the cost of the rehabilitation is at least 25 percent of the value of the property when purchased. This detail means that the program "tends to encourage rehabilitation of properties that need a substantial amount of work or are not located in strong housing markets."[19] In Baltimore this includes former factories or warehouses or other large buildings that require radical and costly transformation to function as residential properties or Baltimore's ubiquitous row houses or other small residential buildings in generally depressed neighborhoods where even modest rehabilitation still costs 25 percent of their purchase value.

Eligible properties must be either an individually designated landmark or a contributing resource within a local or national historic district. A developer might secure individual designation for a significant property, such as the American Can factory or other former industrial buildings that Struever has redeveloped for housing. Otherwise, the building must be related to the particular style or styles that characterized the historic merit of a district when it was designated, contributing to the neighborhood's historic appearance and integrity.

According to the Baltimore Commission for Historic and Architectural Preservation,

> to date, more than 3,300 rehabilitation projects have participated. . . . over $850 million has been invested in historic properties since 1997, with more than 2,000 restorations currently underway in historic districts throughout the City. When these restorations are complete they will result in an additional $800 million in investment, resulting in a total investment amount of $1.5 billion.[20]

Eric Holcomb, executive director of CHAP, says that most work supported by tax credits, in numbers of applications if not total dollars invested, is done by small developers for sale to individual homeowners.[21] Baltimore Heritage, the primary preservation nonprofit, agrees although they assess the numbers somewhat differently.

The state of Maryland has additional tax incentive programs for historic preservation that affect Baltimore.[22] The Maryland Heritage Structure Rehabilitation Tax Credit Program has reportedly "facilitated the redevelopment" of 407 historic commercial structures between 1997 and 2009. "Those projects involved over $923.0 million in total rehabilitation spending . . . by developers, assisted by an investment of $213.9 million in state tax credits." The program also "assisted in the rehabilitation of 2,351 historic residential structures . . . over $201.4 million in total rehabilitation spending . . . assisted by . . . $41.6 million in state tax credits."[23] Reviews of the tax credit program emphasize the multiplier effect many of these projects have had in encouraging further investment, particularly in Baltimore. The use of this credit (and the unpredictable expense to the state) has been overwhelmingly concentrated in Baltimore, creating political complications for state legislators and leading them to curtail the funds budgeted for the credit, thus diminishing its impact.[24]

The structure of state credits makes them less likely to facilitate significant change in declining Baltimore neighborhoods or to serve the interests of low-income residents. They are more likely to help sustain existing stable areas. Rather than providing a transferable credit against increases in postrehabilitation value, this program provides a credit against income for expenses incurred maintaining a historic structure over and above $5,000. To use the state tax credit requires having more than $5,000 available to spend on maintenance and paying significant income tax.

To explore the role Baltimore's HTC might have in driving change in historic districts, I secured district-by-district data from 1996 through 2016 about the use of the credit from Eli Pousson, director of Preservation and Outreach at Baltimore Heritage. I matched Pousson's data with the data set of key demographic characteristics in historic districts and never-designated neighborhoods that I have drawn upon here. I was able to link the use of the credit, both in terms of the number of credit-supported rehabilitation projects and the magnitude of each project, to the racial makeup, median income, and educational attainment of the population of Baltimore historic districts.

I expected to find that the HTC would be more intensively used in Whiter, more educated, higher-income neighborhoods because the benefits of similar programs have historically been unequally distributed in favor of the privileged population. I hypothesized that the data would reveal a distinct negative correlation between the HTC (both its frequency in a district and the magnitude of the investment) and neighborhood disadvantage, manifested as low household income, low educational attainment, and high percent Black. This would be consistent with a recent study by the Preservation Green Lab and Urban Land Institute that asserted that the HTC is "less frequently used in low and moderate income neighborhoods."[25] They attribute this difference to a lack of local capacity to take advantage of the credit; that is, the neighborhood residents lack the wealth to make qualifying investments and the knowledge or skills to apply for the credit (effectively the inverse of my claims about the "institutional capital" of the earliest HDs).[26]

I could find no such correlation in the data available to me. Despite a fine-grained analysis, including numerous demographic variables over significant time periods and detailed HTC data, I found no evidence that the demographic characteristics of a neighborhood had any predictive relationship to the number or magnitude of the approved HTC investments in that neighborhood. The absence of a statistically significant correlation is not dispositive, but it suggests that there is more to the story. This is frankly a surprising finding of no finding.

The one variable in the data that seemed to distinguish neighborhoods from one another was median investment per project: the total dollar amount invested in the rehabilitation of

TABLE 2.4 HTC MEDIAN INVESTMENT PER PROJECT
CLUSTERS, 1996-2016

Project Clusters	Projects Median	Projects Range	Investment/ Project Median	Investment/ Project Range
Low (8)	2.50	1–4	$61,093	$31,875–$87,353
Average (12)	75.50	3–530	$179,590	$150,452–$218,644
High (8)	57.00	1–163	$441,161	$431,414–$804,793

eligible structures in a district between 1996 and 2016, divided by the number of such projects approved for the credit in that district over the same period (table 2.4). When I calculated median investment per project, three distinct groups of historic districts emerged: low (eight), average (twelve), and high (eight) investment per project.[27] The districts within each group are quite similar by this measure and quite different from the districts in the other groups, although they are less like one another by other measures (demography, in particular, but also number of projects). These numbers are for the entire twenty-year period.

The low investment value/project districts are mostly small, residential neighborhoods of moderately priced houses, and the investment value/project seems appropriate to significant renovations. The average investment value/project districts are more difficult to interpret because of the radical variation in number of projects, but they confirm investment in neighborhood transition. In Canton, the 530-project outlier, Zillow estimated the average home price at $312,000 in June 2018. Thus the nearly $180,000 investment value/project suggests the wholesale redevelopment of small, brick row houses for upper-middle-class homebuyers was distorted by a few large projects in the neighborhood. Patterson Park/Highlandtown, with 324 projects and a Zillow-estimated $211,000 home value in June 2018, adjacent to Canton, suggests a similar trend further distorted by some large projects. The majority of certified projects supported by the credit in this group are in these two districts.

Finally, among the high investment value/project districts, Fells Point and Mount Vernon had the greatest number of projects and are two of the more expensive, long-designated, stable neighborhoods in the city, both subject to less change than Canton but to lots of ongoing investments. Nevertheless, the $441,161 median investment/project is a puzzlingly large number. There are $2-million townhouses in Mount Vernon that might explain such an investment, but not many of them. The aggregate nature of the data conceals variation among projects in a district, encouraging further investigation.

Two additional tendencies are worth noting about these groups of historic districts. First, there is a geographic tendency; high value per project neighborhoods tend to be just outside the central business district and follow a spine up toward Johns Hopkins University's main campus. They include some of the first neighborhoods to designate as historic districts (Fells Point, Bolton Hill) and some of the areas most transformed over the period for which I have data (Charles Village/Abell, a gentrifying "arts district," Hampden). Average value per project neighborhoods fall in a ring around the center but are a bit farther out. They are mostly residential neighborhoods and range from early (Federal Hill) and more suburban districts (Guilford, Roland Park, Tuscany-Canterbury), to gentrified, White, working-class neighborhoods (Canton, Patterson Park/Highlandtown), and to more complicated neighborhoods that combine redevelopment with continued disadvantage (Union Square, Old West Baltimore). Low value per project neighborhoods are scattered well outside the city center in effectively suburban neighborhoods, including Original Northwood. This suggests that HTC investment value is related to the geography of density and institutional involvement and focuses on other drivers of revitalization.[28]

Second, I want to highlight the *absence* of any profound tendencies. In a radically segregated city, whether by race or income, the distribution and concentration of HTC investment follows no particular, discernable pattern. It does not reinforce segregation by race or income, although it may not weaken it either. It is difficult to identify another urban development resource that operates this way in relation to segregation and inequality.

MINIMAL CORRELATION AND NEIGHBORHOOD MATCHING

My correlation analysis of Baltimore neighborhoods, historically designated and otherwise, revealed little more. There was no consistent relationship between historic designation and other variables across all neighborhoods, confirming the variation we have already seen. The strongest relationships were among the demographic status variables themselves, again confirming something we already knew about neighborhoods. Whiteness predicts future Whiteness in a neighborhood more powerfully than the other status variables, but educational attainment and income are still both pretty good predictors of those variables in future observations. The demographic composition of a Baltimore neighborhood, at least as measured by individual characteristics, is best explained by what it was like in the recent past, although even the more distant past explains it pretty well. This effectively reiterates Sampson's "enduring neighborhood effect"[29]—that neighborhoods influence the population that inhabits them—and the strong continuity of neighborhood demographics, independent of the historic status of neighborhoods. Districts like Original Northwood, in which significant change occurs according to one demographic measure but not the others, are the exceptions.

Moderate correlations *between* status variables suggest that higher status and disadvantage compound (again, something we knew from Sampson and others who have shown this more comprehensively), but demographic characteristics of neighborhoods do not predict one another very reliably in a city as diverse as Baltimore. Baltimore is a majority Black city with significant Black middle and upper-middle classes, but it also has significant working-class and poor White populations. There are too many possible combinations of race, educational attainment, and income for correlations among these measures to be very strong.

The association between race and educational attainment is particularly interesting because it points to the way these associations change over time. In the earliest part of the period for which I have data, when there was a larger White working-class contingent in Baltimore, race and educational attainment were only weakly related—there may have been slightly more Whites than Blacks with college degrees but plenty of both without. By 2010, the correlation coefficient approaches 0.7, suggesting that the Whites who remained or moved in, as working-class Whites continued to leave the city through the end of the twentieth century, were highly educated. This seems obvious from my earlier discussion of Downtown, but it also appears to be true in Mount Vernon, Charles Village/Abell (near Johns Hopkins University), North Central (just to the north of Mount Vernon, near the Amtrak station, and a recent arts district), and Patterson Park/Highlandtown (adjacent to gentrified Canton and rapidly changing itself). This also suggests a kind of polarization; as the association strengthens, the contrast intensifies between Whiter neighborhoods with greater human and cultural capital and disadvantaged Black neighborhoods.

There are also a few notably weak or negative associations among variables that reinforce some of the other things we have already learned about Baltimore or might have guessed. First, race was not and still is not a good predictor of income in Baltimore. The correlation, or lack thereof, between Whiteness and median household income might be surprising at first glance given what we know generally about the relationship between race and income in the United States. Upon reflection, however, it makes more sense. Baltimore is a city with a historical working-class White population, and over the past fifty years it has become majority Black but also more economically diverse.

This also indirectly contributes to a classic gentrification story about neighborhoods attracting White in-movers with lots of cultural capital but without much money. The newcomers seem to have significant education but are not high earning, suggesting they are recent college graduates, probably without children yet, in creative jobs rather than conventionally remunerative ones, seeking the kinds of urban amenities these neighborhoods provide, and relatively tolerant of risk. More even than just a gentrification story, this may be neighborhood revitalization driven by Richard Florida's "creative class."[30]

Taking Stock and Clarifying
What Remains Unclear

Historic neighborhoods in Baltimore are different from never-designated neighborhoods; they are higher status. They cluster by designation date and group by HTC investment per project. The designation clusters tell us stories of higher status leading to designation and designation preceding status change, with variability reinforced by the distinctive and different stories of Downtown and Original Northwood. Density and local institutional capacity seem related to use of the HTC, at least with regard to the magnitude of investments. Finally, correlation analysis tells us only a little bit more: that neighborhoods are generally consistent over time in their demographic characteristics; that Baltimore has gentrified and polarized, at least in places; and that historic district designation has more recently become a factor in a broader range of neighborhoods.

One further way of considering the influence of historic district designation is to compare neighborhoods that are similar at baseline and observe their trajectories after one designates and the others do not. My data made possible two sets of comparisons like this, one between HDs in the early 1980s designation cluster and the other between HDs in the early 2000s cluster, and never-designated districts similar in 1980 and 2000, respectively. In the 1980s cluster, there are three kinds of HDs: working-class White (96 percent White and approximately 2 percent BA+), majority White (70+ percent) with moderate educational attainment (6 percent BA+),[31] and majority White and highly educated (25–30 percent BA+). In the 2000s cluster, there are also three kinds of HDs: majority Black, poor and poorly educated neighborhoods; working-class White neighborhoods; and majority White highly educated neighborhoods. Having only 2010 data makes distinguishing trends for the 2000s cluster difficult, but distinctions are possible.

Working-class White Canton is similar to four never-designated neighborhoods in 1980 (Brooklyn, Mill Hill, Morrell Park, and Oaklee). From 1980, the year of its designation, until 2010, Canton declined in White population from 98.5 percent to 88.7 percent. The other four neighborhoods declined much more, with Brooklyn and Mill Hill becoming majority Black. Income increased in the never-designated neighborhoods by factors of two to five over thirty years, and in Canton income increased by a factor of six: from the middle of the pack to $72,901 in 2010, almost twice the citywide median of $39,346. Most remarkable are the education numbers; the never-designated neighborhoods change either slightly or hardly at all, with the best educated of the four increasing to 11.6 percent in 2010 (well below the citywide 25.2 percent), remaining working-class neighborhoods or increasingly disadvantaged ones (figure 2.7). Canton, in contrast, has increased in educational attainment by 2,100 percent to 56.7 percent BA+, roughly twice the national average and more than twice the citywide average.[32] Working-class White Canton clearly gentrifies after it designates, in contrast to Brooklyn, Mill Hill, Morrell Park, and Oaklee, which do not designate and do not attract the same higher-status population. These descriptive

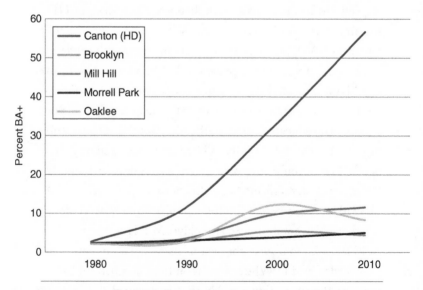

FIGURE 2.7 Educational attainment change over time in one historic district and four never-designated similar neighborhoods, 1980–2010

data cannot attribute causality to designation, but it certainly suggests that designation was a factor.

Butcher's Hill (68.3 percent) and Union Square (77.4 percent), both HDs, are predominantly White without being quite as exclusively so as Canton. Irvington (62.8 percent) and Beechfield (77.2 percent) are similarly White, but are never-designated neighborhoods. All four neighborhoods had educational attainment rates in the range of 5.7 percent to 6.7 percent in 1980. Irvington and Beechfield lost more of their White population faster than Union Square, declining to 10.3 percent White and 9.8 percent White, respectively. Union Square lost two-thirds of its White population, but remained 27 percent White in 2010. Butcher's Hill declined in White population in 1990 and 2000, but increased to 69.9 percent White in 2010, just above its 1980 percentage.

Both of the HDs gain significantly in educational attainment between 1980 and 2010 (figure 2.8). Union Square increased to

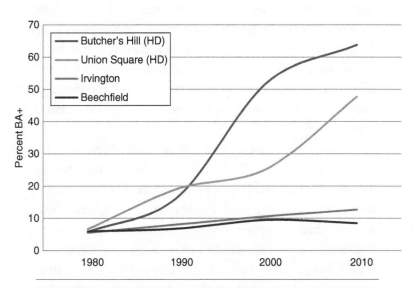

FIGURE 2.8 Educational attainment change over time in two historic districts and two never-designated similar neighborhoods

47.7 percent BA+ (including a big jump from 2000 to 2010), and Butcher's Hill reached 63.8 percent BA+, increasing most between 1990 and 2000. The never-designated neighborhoods increase somewhat, to 12.7 percent and 8.5 percent. In income, the never-designated neighborhoods increased less from a higher initial observation. Union Square increased steadily, and Butcher's Hill jumped way ahead to $88,947 in 2010, much the highest in this matched group. Butcher's Hill, like Canton, appears to be a working to lower-middle-class White neighborhood that has gentrified to become an upper-middle-class White neighborhood following designation. Perhaps not coincidentally, Butcher's Hill and Canton are across Patterson Park from one another in East Baltimore.

Union Square is more complicated: still substantially, although minority, White. It is integrated, pretty well-educated, and middle-income for Baltimore. Although not obviously gentrified, it is clearly improved by standard measures of class. In-person observation of Union Square also points to how these geographies are complex, even at the neighborhood scale: the square for which the neighborhood is named, a nineteenth-century park, is surrounded by grand, well-maintained, three-story brick townhouses with Priuses parked out front (figure 2.9), whereas two blocks away the neighborhood seems abandoned (figure 2.10).[33]

The last group to discuss within these matched groups is predominantly White; it is integrated and middle to upper-middle class by education, mostly better earning, but not at the extreme. The historically designated neighborhoods of Charles Village and Abell (contiguous and near the main campus of Johns Hopkins University) are less distinct from the never-designated neighborhoods of Kernewood and Cheswolde (both further north toward the outskirts of the city) than most of the other

FIGURE 2.9 Union Square (photo by author)

FIGURE 2.10 Near Union Square (photo by author)

HDs are with their comparable neighborhoods. All four decline in White population, from 10 percent to 20 percent, between 1980 and 2010. Educational attainment increased significantly in two of the HDs and one of the never-designated neighborhoods, but it declines in the other. The HDs are pretty low earning (perhaps high cultural capital, low earning creative, near a recent arts district), particularly in contrast to the never-designated neighborhoods, which improve in income substantially over time. This suggests that designation has a less profound effect on already relatively higher-status neighborhoods.

2000s Clusters

In the cluster of HDs that designated in the early 2000s, a number of historic neighborhoods match with never-designated ones: overwhelmingly Black, poor, and poorly educated; working-class White (two groups with slightly different levels of education); and majority White, highly educated. With only 2010 data after the 2000 baseline, the conspicuously disadvantaged neighborhoods show no pattern postdesignation in comparison to their never-designated counterparts, suggesting that whatever designation might accomplish in some circumstances it is not enough to overcome decades of discrimination and disinvestment.

The highest-status group of neighborhoods within this cluster (high White, high educational attainment) is somewhat more interesting because a comparison between HDs and never-designated neighborhoods suggests that historic designation contributes to accelerating positive status change. Both neighborhood types decline somewhat in percent White between 2000 and 2010, remaining close to 80 percent, but the HDs go from an average of 64 percent BA+ in 2000 to 81 percent in 2010, with the never-designated neighborhoods increasing from 63 percent to 69 percent. Similarly, the median household income in the HDs increases from slightly higher in 2000 to 47 percent higher in 2010. Although this is not a strictly consistent effect among already high-status neighborhoods, high-status HDs seem to improve on two critical status measures faster than never-designated neighborhoods: educational attainment and income.

The working-class White neighborhoods within the 2000s cluster seem to follow the patterns observed in the 1980s matched group: the HDs lost less White population than the never-designated neighborhoods and increased educational attainment more. Income in the 2000s HDs increased substantially, from moderate to moderately higher, and again it is all over the place in the never-designated neighborhoods.

Conclusions from Matching Data

Historic designation seems to enhance educational attainment in the context of already relatively high-status neighborhoods (Whiter and wealthier). Historic designation also seems to interact with working-class White neighborhoods to facilitate gentrification, at least in terms of the in-movement of more educated Whites. The relationships between historic designation and race and income are less clear.[34] Finally, the differences between the matched groups of neighborhoods designated in the 1980s and those designated in the 2000s suggests that the shifting purpose of historic designation (perhaps from endogenous, neighborhood self-protection to exogenous revitalization) incorporates more neighborhoods that are less like one another later in the process.

CONCLUSION

We can set aside any concerns that HD designation and neighborhood change have nothing to do with one another. Historic neighborhoods in Baltimore are different from never-designated neighborhoods in that they have higher-status populations. Numerous examples discussed in this chapter suggest that gentrification follows designation in some cases (particularly in working-class White neighborhoods in Baltimore). In Canton, in particular, we see a neighborhood in which class status, as measured by educational attainment, skyrocketed after designation, transforming the neighborhood into one dominated by professionals.

But time and again we also see data suggesting that designation follows status in both longtime high-status neighborhoods, such as the earliest HDs, and in neighborhoods that have experienced recent increases in status, particularly as measured by educational attainment. In all but the most recent cluster of HDs, in fact, the rates of educational attainment in the cluster far exceeded that of the rest of the city *prior* to designation. Sometimes this looks like designation locking in recent status gains in gentrifying neighborhoods, and sometimes this looks more like fortification, using designation as one more defensive strategy of historically high-status neighborhoods.

My sense of causal variation is reinforced by the distinctive and different stories of Downtown and Original Northwood and is compounded by observations about the influence of the Historic Tax Credit. Designation seems to play a role in both anomalous HDs, but a different role, particularly with regard to race. Density and local institutional capacity seem related to use of the HTC, at least with regard to the magnitude of investments. But HTC use seems not to correlate with anything else, which leaves us with additional questions.

Finally, historic district designation and neighborhood change clearly interact in a contingent and contextual fashion, varying radically in their effects across different moments in time and across demographically different neighborhoods, even within a single city. Historic districts in Baltimore are demographically different from never-designated parts of the city, and they change differently both before and after designation. But the reason they are different varies radically from case to case.

As I indicated throughout the chapter, none of the quantitative analyses undertaken here decisively demonstrate a causal relationship, just as prior research had failed to do. Nevertheless, causal relationships seem likely. I have observed intense relationships between high-status neighborhoods and designation (fortification), between working-class White neighborhoods and designation (gentrification), and between educational attainment and designation more generally. The intentionality and conviction of preservation advocates Eric Holcomb and Johns Hopkins and others about the role of preservation in Baltimore also reinforces my suspicion.

The relationships between designation and neighborhood change in Baltimore are variable and seem to be impossible to fully investigate quantitatively. Some answers to these questions lie in the explanations of their actions by participants in these processes. Do highly educated, White in-movers to traditionally working-class neighborhoods articulate designation's role (or at least the neighborhood's history) in their choice of the neighborhood? Do the residents of high-status historic neighborhoods explain their pursuit of designation in terms of neighborhood defense? These questions provide good directions for future research.

A new set of relationships is emerging in Baltimore as designation extends to poorer and Blacker neighborhoods throughout the city. As these relationships produce observable data, we will know to look for the influence of educational attainment, location in the city, density, and institutional capacity. But new factors may also emerge. Finally, I can carry the fundamental lessons of the multiplicity of Baltimore cases into other cities, attentive to context and contingency.

3

MITIGATING GENTRIFICATION
THROUGH PRESERVATION
IN CENTRAL BROOKLYN

I f Baltimore, a legacy city, is at one end of a spectrum of development pressure on historic neighborhoods and housing affordability concerns, Brooklyn, New York, is at the other end of that spectrum. Although New York City's population declined between 1950 and 1970 by more than 800,000 people, it quickly returned to growing, surpassing its previous record population by the year 2000 and continuing on an upward trajectory. It experienced midcentury White flight and deindustrialization, too, but remade itself as a "global city"[1] with an emphasis on finance, fashion, media, and advertising. Unlike Baltimore, New York City has continued to attract large numbers of immigrants from all over the world, which has broadened racial diversity and increased inequality.

As the population of the city as a whole rebounded and the number of well-paying jobs on Wall Street and in Midtown Manhattan increased, newcomers and New Yorkers with money moved farther away from traditional high-status neighborhoods (such as the Upper East Side) and into the outer boroughs. Major parts of Brooklyn had been redlined in the second half of the twentieth century, and banks would not lend to buy or improve properties there. This left gaps between current and potential value as demand for housing increased around them. Some believe these gaps triggered gentrification,[2] but gentrification explanations that rely on consumer preference are relevant for these historic neighborhoods as well, which are defined by Brooklyn's generous, brownstone townhouses. These homes were preserved by those to whom they had been abandoned in the face of disinvestment, maintaining their historical integrity in the absence of lending for home improvement that might otherwise have altered them. Regardless of the cause, Brooklyn has gentrified with increasing momentum.

Historic landmarking played a role in the gentrification of Brooklyn in the 1960s—a process that began in Brooklyn Heights, a neighborhood overlooking southern Manhattan from across the East River.[3] In the 1970s, gentrification spread to Park Slope[4] and Cobble Hill, then Boerum Hill,[5] and on into Williamsburg and Greenpoint and other neighborhoods nearest Manhattan. Most recently, gentrification has reached Prospect Heights, Crowns Heights North, and Bedford-Stuyvesant.

In this chapter, I contrast the processes of historic preservation in central Brooklyn with those in Baltimore to more fully explore the range of relationships between historic district designation and neighborhood change. In doing so, I focus on three neighborhoods: Prospect Heights, Crown Heights, and Bedford-Stuyvesant. These neighborhoods have recently undertaken landmark districting, situating their experience in the larger history of preservation in Brooklyn and the greater New York City area. All three are characterized by late-nineteenth-century residential architecture, predominantly the brownstone townhouse, which are not as grand as the mostly Federalist brick structures of Brooklyn Heights but are stylistically continuous with Park Slope. All three transitioned to majority Black in the decades after World War II, but they are different from one another in terms of recent immigrants and the intensity of poverty. My focus on these neighborhoods permits me to explore the relationship between historic preservation and neighborhood change with the champions of preservation efforts there.

In central Brooklyn, a range of related preservation efforts are taking place in the context of conspicuous and rapid gentrification. Unlike Baltimore, in Brooklyn gentrification pressure clearly precedes landmark districting, undermining the conventional account of preservation causing neighborhood change. However, and as in Baltimore, there is significant variation even among my featured neighborhoods, despite similar gentrification pressures. In Baltimore I investigated the potential relationship between historic district designation and neighborhood change across various neighborhoods, whereas in central Brooklyn I examine the relative consistency of designation as a response to certain neighborhood change despite neighborhood variation.

It is also notable that Baltimore preservation efforts were a top-down urban policy using the historic tax credit and more recent historic districting, whereas landmarking in central Brooklyn appears to be bottom-up. Landmarking is the only tool many local residents feel they have at their disposal to intervene in urban processes that are substantially beyond their control. Afraid of rapid neighborhood change in a city where competition for housing is intense and affordability is often a concern, many homeowners latch on to historic preservation as a way to both influence development in their community and to secure their home's value.

Whereas district designation is used in Baltimore to channel revitalization funding, threats to the historic integrity of central Brooklyn neighborhoods inspire a reaction that brings people together to defend the built environment. The effort to designate landmark districts, in turn, produces an important indirect or secondary effect: community cohesion and a mutual sense of accountability to the neighborhood. Beyond simply designating, the ongoing defense of the neighborhood requires the vigilance of committed local volunteers (see chapter 5). These collective, community-building efforts have additional effects on the trajectories of neighborhoods. Indirect effects in both cities are integral to my research, revealing how historic preservation regulation is one of the only urban policy interventions that makes local control over the built environment possible and, accordingly, how it is caught up in processes beyond those for which it was designed.

In Prospect Heights, for example, landmarking was an effort led primarily by Whites who had moved into a quiet, integrated neighborhood in the 1990s and were loath to see it change around them and watch their neighbors, many of them longtime Black homeowners, get displaced. All of my Prospect Heights interviewees (all White) evince a sensitivity to living in a heavily historically Black neighborhood and talk about working to make connections with longer-time residents as they organized their landmarking efforts—they are somewhat conflicted about their roles in the process of change they see going on around them.

In Prospect Heights we see how major projects perceived as threats to the neighborhood—such as Atlantic Yards (an arena development with thousands of units of housing and office space adjacent)—can accelerate processes of change and spur communities to action. Historic designation was a critical tool for these residents to manage the impact of a major urban development project that would otherwise be beyond their control. That said, as in Baltimore, the civic capacity of individuals in the neighborhood is critical to the success of such efforts.

All of the leaders with whom I spoke are working professionals. To the degree that historic or landmark district designation and the policing of historic preservation rules rely substantially on local residents, local civic capacity shapes their ability to influence local policy and politics.

In Crown Heights the effort to gain historic designation was spearheaded by Denise Brown-Puryear and Deborah Young, founders of the Crown Heights North Association. Both are Black and Brooklyn born and raised, although not exclusively in Crown Heights North itself. Brown-Puryear's interest in the neighborhood was motivated by homeownership and by dealing in real estate, and Young was a new homeowner when they first met. Brown-Puryear also had a copy of the 1978 Landmarks Preservation Commission report on Crown Heights, which facilitated their landmarking effort of the early 2000s. Suzanne Spellen, a devoted preservationist and new homeowner in the neighborhood in 2000, but a relative outsider, reinforced their efforts early in this process. Like Brown-Puryear and Young, she is a Black woman in her middle years. The same can be said about Ethel Tyus, a neighbor and an attorney who had deeper ties to the neighborhood, who helped them create the nonprofit Crown Heights North Association.

The Crown Heights North landmarking experience introduces the obstacle of the "property rights crowd." These homeowners were reluctant to give up complete control over their property, whether they had plans or the wherewithal to exercise it or not. These homeowners had to be persuaded of the overall benefits of preservation before the designation of the neighborhood could proceed. The Crown Heights North story also reiterates the significance of a watershed moment for galvanizing preservation efforts, such as the Atlantic Yards in Prospect Heights or the "highway wars" in Baltimore. In this case, it was the threatened demolition of the 1853 Elkins House, the oldest house still standing in the neighborhood, that brought the property rights crowd around and jumpstarted the landmarking process.

In Bedford-Stuyvesant (Bed-Stuy), rapid neighborhood transition—particularly the influx of young White professionals and the luxury apartment development that follows them (or draws them in?)—has brought residents of all kinds, old-timers and newcomers, together in a frantic effort to intervene in whatever way they could. This took the form of landmark district designation and expansion, facilitated by consultation with their neighbors in Crown Heights North and enforced by the ad hoc Landmarks Committee of the local community board, the self-designated gatekeeper for alterations to buildings within the Bed-Stuy landmark districts. Residents remain panicked by the pace of change they see around them, and they are working hard to mitigate it even as they recognize the limits of preservation regulation to effect the kind of control they seek. Moreover, from my observations the interracial tension that often surrounds gentrification is most prominent in Bed-Stuy.[6]

My portrait of historic preservation in central Brooklyn highlights the ways that the process functions differently in a hot real estate market than in a legacy city despite their shared histories of midcentury deindustrialization, White flight, and redlining. Within central Brooklyn and during a single time period, the neighborhoods still vary from one another just as they did in Baltimore. This suggests that historic preservation is not specific to context at the level of the city but varies with the dynamics of particular neighborhoods. Finally, the qualitative data from Brooklyn provide a window into the understandings, intentions, and experiences of local preservation advocates. The commitment of these amateur volunteers to the built environment they see around them is a critical driver of the preservation process. Brooklyn's distinct experience with historic preservation reinforces the variability of preservation's effects. At the same time, similarities with Baltimore's experiences highlight essential characteristics of the phenomenon, primarily the designation effort as the basis of community organization.

LANDMARKING IN NEW YORK CITY

New York City, like Baltimore, has local regulations that define historic preservation efforts. These regulations were written in an era when concerns about preserving property value were paramount, but they are routinely being applied in a context in which development threatens to reconstruct historic neighborhoods. As noted in Baltimore, federal preservation regulation is relatively toothless. A listing on the National Register of Historic Places only protects property from demolition by federally funded projects and grants tax incentives only for the maintenance of income-producing buildings, rarely individual homes. In New York City, there is little need to incentivize development, so the relevant regulation for our purposes is the city's.

A citywide preservation statute emerged from the late-1950s efforts of residents of Brooklyn Heights to save that neighborhood from redevelopment under Robert Moses, a midcentury reshaper of much of the city.[7] The statute created the Landmarks Preservation Commission (LPC) and gave it the power to determine the fate of historic landmarks and landmark districts in New York. Contributing buildings in landmark districts are protected from demolition or significant alteration, and all efforts to do so must get approval from the LPC, which relies on local neighborhood organizations and community board committees to advise it on the merit of requests. The districts are substantially policed from the street by their residents. As in Baltimore, New York City's historic preservation institutional ecosystem is characterized by a government bureaucracy: the LPC, which is responsible for designation decisions and the enforcement of preservation regulations, and a variety of nonprofit preservation advocates, foremost is the Historic Districts Council (or HDC) followed by the Landmarks Conservancy and the Municipal Art Society.

I begin by letting the major players from these institutions describe the landmarking process, the institutional ecosystem, and the role of preservation in New York. The organizational ecology in New York City is appropriately more complex than that of Baltimore. Their accounts provide the larger historical context through which we can understand the experiences of my three neighborhood case studies.

The Landmarks Preservation Commission

Tenzing Chadotsang was director of outreach and senior preservationist at the New York City LPC from 2004 to 2013.[8] He characterized the LPC as responsive rather than proactive with regard to landmarking; that is, the LPC, and his office in particular, acted on requests from communities to evaluate historical merit and assess the potential for landmark districts rather than surveying the city to seek out historical structures.

Chadotsang described the community and technical side of the process, which is played out in the cases discussed by neighborhood preservation activists below. The typical first step is a request to LPC from a neighborhood group. In response, the LPC research team visits the neighborhood to assess the merit of the proposed district and map and inventory the structures.[9]

After confirmation of historical merit, LPC hosts a stakeholder meeting (local homeowners, businesses, institutions, etc.) to establish the boundaries of the district, which depend on buy-in and pushback.

Further outreach follows this initial stakeholder meeting to confirm that all interested parties are consulted and have a chance for public comment. LPC facilitates multiple community meetings to discuss the process of designation and its consequences, to allow residents to voice their opinions, and to explain landmark regulations and how they will affect any changes property owners might be considering. Chadotsang and his team were actively involved in two of the central Brooklyn neighborhoods I discuss: Crown Heights North and Bedford-Stuyvesant.

Chadotsang described LPC's reception by communities as "a mixed bag." Neighborhoods are often organized before LPC gets there, but he said that they have not always completely understood the consequences of the process in which they are engaged. He recounted that LPC got a lot of support in Crown Heights North because the Crown Heights North Association had already done extensive outreach, including rallying the local city councilperson to the cause. Crown Heights North was "evolving" fast, and a number of triggers—such as historic buildings like the Elkins House being under threat—got the community moving.[10]

In Bed-Stuy an extension to the 1971 Stuyvesant Heights landmark district was proposed in the early 1990s, but it lay dormant for lack of community initiative or support from the LPC. It was eventually taken up by Claudette Brady and others in 2009, in combination with a newly proposed Bedford Corners district.[11] Brady and her group of volunteers pushed to get others in the neighborhood on board and reengaged with the LPC in 2010, and they recruited their local city councilperson, Albert

Vann. This kind of work from the community made Chadot-sang's job much easier: the LPC did not have to track every-one down—the local group had already done it for them. The Stuyvesant Heights expansion was approved in 2013, and the Bedford Corners district was approved in 2015.

Outreach never produced perfect comprehension of the out-comes of the landmarking process, no matter how many com-munity meetings were held. Chadotsang remarked that local residents never seemed to quite understand what they were agreeing to give up. In particular, he worried that many do not comprehend the degree to which landmarking involves giving up property rights. "Landmarking is a [legal] *taking*," he explained, "you give up rights" to your property and lose the ability to make major stylistic changes to the exterior or an expansion.[12] Nev-ertheless, Chadotsang acknowledged that community members have no other tools to manage the change going on around them and that landmarking grants communities significant control. In some neighborhoods, change is so abrupt that landmarking is not possible because the buildings that might have merited pres-ervation are already gone.

When I asked how conscious LPC employees were about their complicity or involvement in local efforts to manage vari-ous kinds of neighborhood change, he said that the LPC was very conscious while he was there. Maintenance that complies with landmark regulation often requires expensive materials and specialist contractors. He and his team had an explicit social justice orientation, and they sometimes discouraged landmark-ing in communities where the costs might become a burden. Chadotsang also implied that he had seen landmarking pro-cesses undertaken with a NIMBY orientation toward lower-income people of color, the flip side of concerns about costs and constraints on change. The implication here is that racist neighborhood defenders might pursue landmarking in the belief that it would raise property values, prevent the kind of alterations that repurpose middle-class housing for lower-income residents, and make homeownership more expensive in addition to consolidating local control. Whether or not landmarking is effective when put to this purpose remains unclear and is an interesting direction for future research.

Chadotsang refused to use the term "gentrifying" with regard to any of the neighborhoods examined here. When I asked about gentrification in Bed-Stuy, a neighborhood I think of as gentrifying quickly in the past ten years, Chadotsang said that "Bed-Stuy is *gone*—maybe East New York is gentrifying."[13] It became clear over the course of our conversation that Chadotsang used "gentrifying" to describe what I would call the tipping point: the earliest moment when new investment or the in-movement of demographically different people began rather than the ongoing process of change. This is notable because even in neighborhoods under gentrification for two decades or more, such as Prospect Heights, one would be unlikely to call the process "complete" (however one chose to define that).

Several themes of the interview with Chadotsang are particularly noteworthy. First, Chadotsang confirmed my growing sense that landmarking tends to spread from one neighborhood to the next. He attributes this to architectural similarities between adjacent neighborhoods, the degree to which neighborhoods share similar styles and similar historic merit. Although this is relevant, Chadotsang did not appear to appreciate the degree to which historic preservation is a social as much as an architectural process, one rooted in overlapping networks and cooperating organizations.

Second, Chadotsang's descriptions of his experiences in various neighborhoods point to how landmarking in New York City is a bottom-up process initiated by community groups. Throughout the interview, he returned to how important community efforts are in building support for landmarking, independent of the LPC. In our conversation, Chadotsang separated the process of outreach and designation into *community and technical issues*, for which he was responsible (concerns and misconceptions around landmarking and design and maintenance issues associated with historic merit), and *political issues*, such as dealing with the local community board and city councilperson, that his colleague Jennie Fernandez handled.

In fact, his distinction between the technical and political aspects of the process is a useful way to distinguish between the aesthetic commitments of neighborhood preservation advocates to a specific vision of historical style and the advocacy necessary to enforce this orthodoxy. Finally, it is notable that Chadotsang, like Holcomb in Baltimore, is conscious of his organization's relationship to neighborhood change, even as he expressed an exaggerated sense of gentrification pressures in Brooklyn.

The Historic Districts Council

Two nonprofit preservation organizations that operate outside the city bureaucracy, the New York Landmarks Conservancy and the Municipal Art Society, do not generally support neighborhood groups or individuals seeking to explore historic designation. For that, there is the Historic Districts Council, which promotes itself as the "Advocate for New York City's Historic Neighborhoods."

Simeon Bankoff is the longtime executive director of the HDC, an organization he described as an independent, citywide, community-oriented, loyal opposition to the Landmarks

Preservation Commission, championing the interests of local communities in the face of city planning practices dominated by the real estate development industry. Bankoff explained their niche in the ecosystem as follows: The Landmarks Conservancy is "careful" and technical, running the largest funding program for preservation with extensive resources, and it "does big stuff [working on historic structures], not advocacy."[14] His views of the Municipal Art Society are less generous, describing it as "academic," preoccupied with questions like "what is the city?," and, thus, less effective in concrete terms.

For Bankoff, landmarking in New York City is a way of empowering local residents "to have a strong voice in determining the physical characteristics of their neighborhoods." He maintained that designation efforts can help mitigate displacement while "creating a neighborhood network, building a classic community group,"[15] nurturing and supporting local businesses, and encouraging stability of ownership. Bankoff conceded that this may increase property values and thus facilitate gentrification. As he pointed out, boosting home values is written into the landmarking law as one justification for the takings to which Chadotsang referred. Still, if landmark designation does increase property values, Bankoff argued that it does so more slowly and with less volatility than speculative development. Like Chadotsang, he conceded that NIMBYism sometimes creeps into these efforts and that neighborhood residents use whatever they can "to frustrate development . . . that is wildly out of scale . . . and the demolition of community centers."[16]

Bankoff, however, dismissed the idea that landmarking *causes* demographic change in New York. He said that "gentrification" [in its relationship to landmarking] is "meaningless, like pornography: you know it when you see it."[17] Although the displacement of lower-income residents of color from many neighborhoods is real, Bankoff appears to mean that the attribution of causes is a matter of perspective, often distorted by other ideological commitments. In his view, neighborhood change is frequently the result of pro-growth forces in New York who "adopt affordable housing as a cloak," giving them cover for the redevelopment of historic areas. Although Bankoff admits there should not be a conflict between affordable housing and historic preservation, he said that the progressive rhetoric around the de Blasio administration's housing plans, which prioritize affordable housing above all other urban policy interventions, is "hard to deal with" from HDC's perspective. He meant, I think, that advocates of preservation are preemptively cast as the enemies of affordable housing (and thus the poor, people of color, etc.) if they resist rezoning and redevelopment, so their preservation arguments are dismissed.

Bankoff and Chadotsang describe the set of circumstances within which my central Brooklyn interviewees operate. They perceive the public agency tasked with approving and enforcing landmark designation as passive, technocratic, no longer proactive, but generally receptive. In contrast, HDC is viewed as a critical facilitator, resource, and advocate for preservation in New York. Everyone, I am told, knows Bankoff, and he knows everybody (this certainly proved true of all of my Brooklyn interviewees). They also perceive the city's landmarking rules as the only accessible tool for managing the changes New Yorkers see in the neighborhoods around them. Unlike Baltimore, they emphasize the view that landmarking efforts are community-building exercises—bottom-up processes that build local political capacity. Finally, they understand that they are operating in a complex landmarking ecology, with efforts spreading from neighborhood to neighborhood, but they are also caught up in political and cultural contests over control of space and place.

With this context in mind, it is time to zero in on the recent landmark districting processes of three central Brooklyn neighborhoods. In each, I explain how residents have attempted to use landmarking regulation to address concerns about neighborhood change (physical and social or cultural). I examined my interviews with preservation advocates in Prospect Heights, Crown Heights North, and Bedford-Stuyvesant for historical detail, motivation, and discourses around historic preservation. I present these accounts in a broader context by interleaving detailed quantitative data on Brooklyn made available by the Furman Center at New York University through their Core-Data.nyc portal. The quantitative data help to confirm and at times to qualify the perceptions of my interviewees about the processes at work in the city around them.

PROSPECT HEIGHTS

I met Mary Shuford in the Prospect Heights brownstone on Sterling Place that she had moved into in 1972. She has recently repurposed the basement or garden level as an independent apartment and moved down there, leaving the upper floors to her daughter, son-in-law, and two granddaughters. I was referred to her because she is a neighborhood preservation advocate involved in the Prospect Heights Neighborhood Development Council, but much of our conversation was dedicated to the recent history of the neighborhood.[18] We sat at a table in her new kitchen to talk, accompanied about half the time by her daughter, Virginia, a woman in her late thirties or early forties who grew up in the house.

Shuford and her husband were the second White couple to move onto the block. At the time, the neighborhood was predominantly middle-class Black homeowners, city workers, for example, and there was minimal turnover. Shuford reported securing a mortgage through a personal connection at Banker's Trust and suggested that was exceptional because "no one was lending" in the neighborhood (this anecdotal account is consistent with the well-known history of redlining in NYC described by Suleiman Osman and others[19]).

As Shuford remembers it, the neighborhood change of the 1960s and 1970s was not as antagonistic a process as the one in the past few decades. There was minimal friction around change, perhaps, she said, because the in-movement of White families was a "trickle." She drew a contrast with Fort Greene, where she remembers tensions in the same period, saying that there was none of that in Prospect Heights, where it was a positive process. Shuford emphasized the strong sense of community in the neighborhood at the time into which newcomers, like herself, were incorporated.

Although the neighborhood had been stable, it started to get "rough" in the late 1970s. Her side of the street, which is made up of three-story brownstones, did not change much, but the large apartment buildings across the street "went to pieces." Even then, she remembers, "this was a good block," people sat on their front steps, chatting and watching the neighborhood. There was a lot of pride in the houses, they were cared for and well-loved. She did say, though, that you had to be aware, as you moved around the neighborhood, of how far you went from home. Her daughter chimed in to emphasize that this concern characterized neighborhood children's experience in particular, that they needed to stay roughly within sight or on the block.

This period, which Shuford described as "blight," went on through the 1980s. The large apartment buildings went empty, and even some of the brownstones were turned to illegal purposes. That said, she reminisced semi-ironically, the crack dealers on the block were "*our* crack dealers," and they acted as "eyes on the street," if complicated ones.

Shuford reported that the turnaround in the neighborhood came with the crime rate drop and the end of the crack epidemic. She did not see this as a particularly local phenomenon but as a citywide one. Shuford also characterized this change in direction as a slow process of improvement, until it gathered momentum. Although more young White people would not begin moving into the neighborhood in significant numbers until the late 1990s, Mary and Virginia agreed that even the early 1990s felt safer. Her sense was that it was not until at least 2010 that significant development extended to the far side of Washington Avenue, which is often considered the boundary with Crown Heights North.[20]

In the mid-1990s, most neighborhood residents were in favor of the neighborhood's perceptible transition, and significant remodeling was resisted. Expansions, in particular, were viewed as selfish because they affected the open space behind the brownstones many people treasured as a retreat. Independent of physical changes, the neighborhood experienced a marked demographic transition in the mid-1990s that Shuford described as a "positive incremental improvement that suddenly accelerated." She and Virginia agree, nevertheless, that many households had been on the block for more than forty years—together they quickly count more than ten who have lived here that long, all Black homeowners. The transition, although substantial, has not been total. Other sources confirm this account of a gradual increase in the White population until about 2000.

Shuford recounted that there was significantly less concern about the neighborhood's trajectory before about 2000 and that no one anticipated the enormous pressure of the last few years. From Shuford's perspective, the turning point was the announcement of the Atlantic Yards project (redevelopment of a defunct railroad yard, including an arena for the Brooklyn Nets NBA team and thousands of units of housing) in the early 2000s and the "destructive development" that quickly followed. She complained that developers showed up and destroyed the "continuity" of Prospect Heights. They were insensitive to neighbors and to the problems they caused for them.

For Shuford, the Prospect Heights Neighborhood Development Council (PHNDC), founded in 2004, was a necessary step to resist the developers' incursions. The landmark designation of Prospect Heights in 2009 proved effective in stopping destructive development and maintaining the visual quality of the neighborhood. More broadly, Shuford has the sense that historic designation stabilizes property values because it encourages maintenance of the property. But rather than being stabilized, she noted that prices shot up in Prospect Heights after landmark designation in a way she described as "mind-boggling." She regrets that the higher values bring a different "tone" to the neighborhood, which is increasingly White and less community oriented.

Gib Veconi is one of the leaders of the landmarking effort in Prospect Heights that began in the early 2000s.[21] At the time of our interview, he was the president of PHNDC, whose Landmarks Committee routinely makes recommendations on changes in the landmark district for approval by the LPC. He is White, a professional, and moved into the neighborhood in the 1990s. Like Shuford, he identified the announcement of the Atlantic Yards project in the early 2000s as adding significant pressure to early, but established, gentrification trends in Prospect Heights. Moreover, like Shuford, he believes it reinforced existing residents' sense of an urgent need to protect the

neighborhood from runaway development. But he also emphasized that efforts to landmark Prospect Heights as a way of con-
trolling change were already underway.

Atlantic Yards is not the whole story in Prospect Heights, but
it is certainly an important part of it, including in a somewhat
unusual way. Veconi alleged that the LPC feels "guilty" about
their passivity, which led to a failure to protect landmarks after
the announcement of the Atlantic Yards project set off redevelopment in the commercial corridors bounding Prospect Heights.
He referred specifically to the Ward Bakery building and a bank
building on Washington Avenue, both of which were torn down
before the local neighbors mobilized for designation. He suggested that LPC's guilt was useful in moving the city landmark
district application along in 2008 and that it is likely to be useful going forward. Prospect Heights received city designation
in 2009, and preservation advocates got the National Register
of Historic Places to expand the national district beyond the
bounds of the city district in 2016. Veconi hopes local advocates
can now "leverage" LPC's guilt to expand the city district to
match the national one.

In Prospect Heights we see a clear instance of gentrification
preceding historic district designation. Veconi, however, drew
attention to the incremental and staged nature of gentrification and maintains that an intermediate stage of gentrification
provided the original trigger for the landmarking effort. By the
mid-1990s, the three-and-a-half-story brownstones that characterize the neighborhood had increased in price in a way that
attracted the attention of small-scale developers. Yet these same
developers felt the need to expand the buildings to produce the
revenue necessary to cover their debt and still profit. Many of
the original brownstones had kitchen extensions on the ground
level (referred to as an "L," as if the letter's base were extending

into the backyard), so the common approach for small developers was to break out the back wall of the upper floors to extend
them out over the ground-level kitchen, and occasionally farther
into the backyard. This approach to expansion enabled the developer to cut the building into three or four reasonable-sized flats,
but the house extended into the open space of the interior block
(what neighborhood residents refer to as "the donut," although
it really is the hole in the donut), which we saw in Shuford's
account was an important attribute of the homes. The expansions also break the common and consistent rear wall of all of
the properties on a block.

Danae Oratowski, a neighbor of Veconi's and fellow Prospect Heights preservation activist, also White and arrived in the
1990s, provided a similar story.[22] She explained that Prospect
Heights brownstones are "under built" in relation to their lots.
Prior to landmark protection, developers could expand without
having to get a zoning variance. Oratowski complained that
developers profited from the historic beauty of the neighborhood
and all the work that homeowners had put into their properties
while building "awful buildings" in Prospect Heights, essentially
free-riding. She claimed that "massive" extensions were boxing
in people in their rear yards and threatening a "Prospect Heights
way of life" that relied on the integrity of the donut [hole] as
an "escape from Manhattan." This comment makes more sense
when one realizes that many Prospect Heights residents were
professionals at that time who worked in Manhattan during the
week, but it also generalizes their experience.

Veconi and Oratowski agree that this visible intrusion into
their space had an immediate impact on their experience, spur-
ring Prospect Heights homeowners to action and galvanizing support for local landmark district designation. Impending
development was no longer an abstract threat but "concrete

examples in the donut," said Oratowski. Veconi attributes preservation's popularity in Prospect Heights to human nature. He
said that people are uncomfortable with development happening next door, people don't like it.

Oratowski described the founding of the PHNDC in 2004
as a way to represent the "community position on Atlantic
Yards" and their needs and concerns. Other organizations were
already organizing around the proposed development, notably
Develop Don't Destroy Brooklyn, which was in vocal opposition, and BUILD, which Oratowski described as an "AstroTurf"
group started by the developers in support of the Atlantic Yards
project. But it was the PHNDC that brought the neighborhood together, uniting local civic associations and appointing
representatives to the board from each of the block associations
within Prospect Heights.

Oratowski recalled that PHNDC did not immediately take a
position on the Atlantic Yards project. It tried to "ascertain community needs" first, so it could represent the range of neighborhood positions. This made some in the neighborhood skeptical
of the organization; they felt it was "a little suspect." Ultimately,
though, Oratowski explained that PHNDC's dedication to
transparency got them past the suspicion.

Oratowski described PHNDC's role with regard to the
Atlantic Yards project as pushing to figure out who is accountable to the community—at the state level and in the developer's
organization. PHNDC has sued twice over the project, winning
a revised or supplemental Environmental Impact Statement
after the timeline for the project was revised and accepting an
accelerated schedule for affordable housing that the developer
had planned to delay. Most recently, the developer changed the
plans for one of the buildings to all office space (from mixed
office and residential), delaying affordable housing again because

the proportion has to be recalculated with the total residential units reduced.

Oratowski also argued that people in the neighborhood had an interest in historic buildings that predated Atlantic Yards. She offered the house tour as evidence. House tours began in the 1990s and were organized by the no-longer-active Prospect Heights Association in response to house tours in nearby Park Slope. The house tours were "a celebration of architecture" and "a community-building gesture." They also addressed the problem that it was a bit hard to get a sense of the neighborhood as a whole at the time: it felt "scattered, sleepy" and "had no center." Significant commercial development has taken place since then on the large streets at the edges of the neighborhood and in a couple of locations in the interior.

Oratowski said that house tours were "reaffirming," demonstrating that people were staying and investing (at a time when change in the neighborhood was conspicuous and somewhat disconcerting). She called the tours mutual "acknowledgment" [of interest in old houses and their rehabilitation, in the neighborhood] and suggested that, in addition to enabling one to see who was living in the neighborhood and into homes, one got to see who else was on the tour and meet likeminded folk. Oratowski also noted that the tours became, in a sense, victims of their own success. Prospect Heights homes became fancy enough through the neighborhood's gentrification that their owners were no longer comfortable opening them up to strangers.

Veconi, more than any of the other interviewees, identified and highlighted the bottom-up nature of historic preservation in Brooklyn and its significance for the social dynamics of the neighborhood. He told me that "historic designation inserts an element of democracy into land use decisions." Rather than a top-down process of bureaucratic approval of individual applications for zoning variances or building permits, the community gets some say with regard to changes to the built environment. Despite whatever landmarking fails to do, it does preserve "character," that nebulous sense of distinctiveness related to the physical coherence and integrity of a neighborhood, by creating a mechanism for generating consensus around character.

By providing an opportunity for collective control or community oversight and by bringing more people into the process, landmark designation and implementation devolve determinations of significance, to some degree, giving more say about appropriate alterations to the people most immediately affected by those changes. Neighborhood residents concerned about preservation have the opportunity to weigh in on all recommendations to the LPC. Preservation is policed from the street level by laypeople, volunteers interested in historic buildings.

Veconi also highlighted the way this process provides a locus for community building, creating a site for community cohesion and reinforcing a mutual sense of accountability to the neighborhood. Although people sometimes hope for more from preservation regulation than it can actually do (a sentiment many of my informants observed), Veconi noted that the process of organizing the neighborhood to pursue city landmark district designation builds the basis of a group to "defend" the neighborhood going forward.

The legal constraints on building in historic districts create *periodic* opportunities for community control and community cohesion rather than one-off events. Once a district has been designated as historic, any property owner seeking to making significant alterations to a building within the Prospect Heights district, for example, must obtain the consent of her neighbors through a petition to the Landmarks Committee of PHNDC. Veconi believes that the petition becomes a "social process" that brings neighbors into conversation and emphasizes PHNDC's "educational role," showing owners how to get LPC approval.

Finally, as we have seen before, advocates of historic preservation in Prospect Heights strongly contest the claim that designation causes gentrification. Veconi, for example, told me that, at least in terms of Prospect Heights' relationship to Atlantic Yards, major rezonings affect the neighborhood more profoundly than landmark district designation. Atlantic Yards had been a Metropolitan Transit Authority train yard and was rezoned to permit twenty- to thirty-story residential towers. Although the housing component of the Atlantic Yards project will take ten to twenty years to complete, including its mandatory affordable units, Veconi suggested that changes to commercial rents and residential property prices in the surrounding area happened immediately following rezoning, thus triggering displacement that cannot realistically be compensated for by eventual residential development. Even the affordable units ultimately constructed will target new residents rather than those displaced or at risk of displacement now because of the pressure the time lag puts on rents.

Veconi conceded that Prospect Heights has changed a great deal, but he argued that historic preservation functions as a countervailing force to the pressures that emerge from a major rezoning. In particular, and here Veconi echoed Jane Jacobs, he believes that preservation slows the loss of existing affordable housing and low-cost commercial real estate by simply preventing their demolition or radical upgrading. Jacobs claims that older buildings are less expensive because they have long internalized the costs of their construction, so they can rent for less unless and until a new round of investment pushes their price upward: preservation maintains a pool of affordable space.[23]

Oratowski also acknowledged demographic changes to the neighborhood but argued that in Prospect Heights these are as much a generational issue as one about race. Most of her African American neighbors are of an older generation, and their children are not staying in the neighborhood, so they have moved to the South and kept their houses as investments. These older Black residents are not as interested in preservation, she said. They are focused on maintaining their own houses but do not really see how landmarking would help the neighborhood and are sensitive to increased costs.

Oratowski was also skeptical of the neighborhood newcomers' orientation to the historic homes they are buying. With the wealth of the newer arrivals comes an absence of sweat equity investment in their homes (a point also made by Shuford). This both changes homeowners' relationship to the houses themselves and removes a key basis of community organization: gardening, sweeping of stoops, and caring for the neighborhood together that were prevalent in the 1970s through the 1990s. Homeowners who no longer do the kind of work that encouraged casual sociability have eroded interaction and the sense of community.

Neighborhood Change and Crime Rates

Before moving on to the experience of historic designation in Crown Heights, I want to situate Shuford's memories of the crime rates in Brooklyn in the 1980s and 1990s and its relationship to the calculations about neighborhoods that urban residents make in choosing to move in or out. Crime rates in New York City have, indeed, been on the decline since the mid-1990s for a multitude of reasons beyond the scope of this project.[24] Perhaps more interesting is the fact that crime rates in central Brooklyn continued to decline in the early 2000s (the period that brought district designation to two of my three neighborhoods), making neighborhoods previously considered too dangerous more appealing to less risk-tolerant individuals.

Figure 3.1 tracks serious crimes per 1,000 residents in central Brooklyn in selected community districts. CoreData.nyc defines serious crimes as "those classified as a major felony as defined by the New York City Police Department," explaining that "serious property crimes include most types of burglary, larceny, and motor vehicle theft," and "serious violent crime includes most types of assault, murder (including nonnegligent manslaughter), rape, and robbery."[25]

The first thing to notice about this figure is the steep and consistent decline in serious crime from 2000 to 2009. Crime

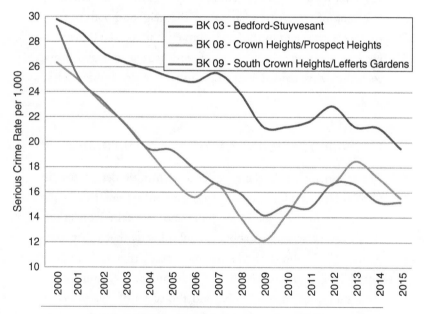

FIGURE 3.1 Serious crimes per 1,000 residents, Brooklyn community districts

Source: NYU Furman Center CoreData.nyc

declined further in Prospect Heights and Crown Heights (54 percent) than in Bed-Stuy (29 percent). Recent research by the Furman Center indicates that the nationwide decline in violent crime since the 1990s, and its particular manifestation in cities, has made the in-movement of high-income, college-educated people to central city neighborhoods, even majority-minority neighborhoods, more likely.[26] Thus declining violent crime can be read as a gentrification indicator that helps explain the consistent increase in educational attainment in central Brooklyn.

The next thing to notice is an uptick in crime rates in 2009. This is a greater than 50 percent increase from the lowest rate in Prospect Heights and Crown Heights North, and an increase of only 8 percent in Bed-Stuy. The increase in crime rates does not track with the longer-term trajectory of neighborhood change (as measured by other indicators), although educational attainment and increases in White population dip briefly in Bedford-Stuyvesant at the same time. This appears to suggest, following the Furman Center researchers, that declines in crime encourage the gentrification of neighborhoods, but once that process is underway, the newcomers are relatively insensitive to increases in the crime rate as long as they remain historically low. These particular changes were probably related to the Great Recession and may be explained away in popular discourse, especially given the more recent return to declining rates.

CROWN HEIGHTS NORTH

Denise Brown-Puryear and Deborah Young founded the Crown Heights North Association (CHNA) in 2002, shortly after moving into the neighborhood, and they spearheaded a landmarking process for the neighborhood that is now in its fourth phase.[27] In 2015, Liz Strong recorded an extensive oral history interview with Brown-Puryear and Young.[28] I draw heavily on that interview in the narrative that follows along with an original interview with Suzanne Spellen, who moved to the neighborhood in 2000, joined CHNA soon after it was founded, and has proven instrumental in promoting preservation in Crown Heights North by leading tours of the historic resources of the neighborhood and writing about them.[29]

Brown-Puryear and Young bought brownstones on the same block of Sterling Place (only blocks from Mary Shuford in Prospect Heights) a few months apart in 2001. They quickly hit it off and discovered that they were "a package . . . the perfect match" in terms of skills and personality. Both were Brooklyn natives and effectively lifelong residents of central Brooklyn, and they had a passion for history and the energy of new homeowners. Young also brought to the table experience working with government, having been employed in the state's bureaucracy in Albany for five years.[30]

Beyond the serendipity of their meeting and productive partnership, Brown-Puryear and Young emphasize (like both Veconi and Bankoff) the ways in which landmark advocacy can become a form of, and often draws upon prior experience with, community activism.[31] In different parts of their oral history of the process, Young said, and Brown-Puryear confirmed, "It was about preservation but it wasn't all about preservation. It was just about being *neighborly*."[32] The landmark district project was always part of a broader sense of community and caring for the neighborhood.[33] As Young put it, "While our core mission was about preservation, that's not the only thing that's important."[34]

Both also explained how the 2000s designation process was facilitated by the fact that Brown-Puryear happened to be in possession of LPC's 1978 survey of the neighborhood. She had participated, as a young person, in the documentation of historic resources in the neighborhood that formed the basis of a claim of "merit," saving the more recent designation effort much of the work that would otherwise have been required. The report was generated because in the 1970s LPC was "mandated" to survey neighborhoods of color to see which were "worthy" of saving, according to Suzanne Spellen.[35] Among the neighborhoods surveyed was Crown Heights, but a historic district was not proposed at the time.

For a variety of reasons, including its status as a majority-Black neighborhood not particularly close to Manhattan and victim of systematic disinvestment for the second half of the twentieth century, Crown Heights was relatively unchanged in 2001. I call this "preservation through malign neglect." Brown-Puryear states:

> The other reason, too, why a lot of these houses remain intact is because people didn't have money to fix them up. People didn't have money to do crazy things on the outside, you know brick facing, put aluminum siding, paint it all kind of funky colors, people didn't have the money to do it. So that was a blessing in disguise.[36]

But things were changing in New York City, and by 2001 Crown Heights was threatened by development. Crime rates in the neighborhood were continuing to fall from their first turn downward in the mid-1990s, and the population of both the borough and the city more generally were increasing, putting new pressure on housing markets and neighborhoods that had not experienced investment in decades.

Brown-Puryear and Young's ability to navigate the administrative process helped them get extensive support from preservation organizations both inside and outside the city government

(LPC and HDC, in particular). They also reported quickly recruiting their local elected officials to the landmark districting cause without too much difficulty.[37] Within the neighborhood, however, they acknowledged that they met resistance. Local homeowners, whom Suzanne Spellen referred to as the "property rights crowd," were skeptical of the process, perhaps because at some level they recognized it for the *legal taking* it is.[38] Young explained their perception:

> They didn't want people telling them what to do with their houses. It was going to increase the cost of homes in the community . . . they were not going to be able to afford to maintain their homes because with your landmark then you have to do certain things, and they could not afford to do those things.

Brown-Puryear conceded that preservation was only one among many concerns for people like these in a changing labor market. Over time these homeowners were persuaded through patient education, many meetings, and outreach that also helped address local neighborhood issues such as predatory lending to elders.[39] As in Prospect Heights, however, their conversion was accelerated by impending development.

In 2006, prior to the landmark district's designation and accompanying protections, the mid-nineteenth-century Elkins House was slated for demolition. When development was so clearly "right in their own backyard," even those who had initially resisted conceded the importance of preservation and got on board. Locals were spurred to action, blockading construction machinery, even getting a "stand-alone designation" for the house from the LPC until the district went through.[40] As a cause, the Elkins House was clearly effective, although it was

valued more for its status as the oldest house in the neighborhood than for any particular aesthetic qualities.[41]

Brown-Puryear concluded by addressing the changes in the
neighborhood that have continued since designation, especially
the challenges of integrating young, White newcomers unaccus-
tomed to living among Black Americans.

> And my concern I guess may be along those lines is that with the
> influx of new residents coming in that there will not be a separat-
> ing but a cohesive mixing, in terms of coming into a neighborhood
> that has that foundation of community awareness *where neighbors*
> *greet each other, speak to other, acknowledging each other as you pass*
> *each other on the street. I notice that that does not happen with the*
> *new incoming folks. It just doesn't. It's like they're in their own world.*
> And that's all well and fine, but you're coming into an established
> community and established neighborhood. . . . So I think that
> sometimes can cause a little uncomfortability, and I think having
> some kind of orientation or something that that group is reached
> out to sort of bring them in and understand.[emphasis added][42]

Suzanne Spellen confirmed much of Brown-Puryear and
Young's account of Crown Heights North in our interview.
Unlike Prospect Heights, where educated White activists, themselves early gentrifiers in a sense, spearheaded a landmarking
process that sought to incorporate many long-time Black residents, designation in Crown Heights North was driven by those
longtime residents or, at least, by people who viewed themselves
as very similar. Spellen emphasized "huge" support from the
general population of homeowners, many of their families in the
neighborhood since the 1940s.[43] The naysayers were just a small
crowd, in her recollection.

Spellen also identified the Elkins House emergency as the threat that galvanized local interest in landmarking. She bragged that local residents persuaded the LPC to designate the house in "record time," saving it from the bulldozer "by an hour." Spellen also emphasized how this experience converted the remaining resistance, including the property rights crowd. People realized, "if we don't do this, this is what can happen"—our buildings will be demolished. Spellen characterized the Crown Heights North district as having "sailed through" the process ahead of Park Slope, confirming Brown-Puryear and Young's sense of enthusiastic engagement with the LPC, although she also suggested that they (CHNA) "really had their stuff together."

Since the initial designation in 2011, the Crown Heights North landmark district has expanded twice, with a fourth part of the neighborhood now awaiting consideration by the LPC. Landmarking has gained locals influence over exterior changes. Spellen argued, like Chadotsang, that landmarking was the only strategy available to neighborhood residents to manage change.

Spellen raised some concerns about the outcome, describing something of a backlash from longtime residents in response to the district's designation. During the Great Recession in 2009 and 2010, she said former Manhattanites who were cash-rich from selling condos before the crash "found" Crown Heights and began to drive prices up. Because landmarking was fresh on everyone's minds, longtime residents misperceived a connection between landmarking and the gentrification that followed.

Like the other historic preservation activists we have heard from, Spellen believes this view is rooted in what she calls a red herring. Spellen argued that there was no causal relationship because landmarking came well before this most recent wave of gentrification. She also noted that recent landmarking did not protect the market in Bed-Stuy from a significant downturn. It "didn't make a darned bit of difference" there. Designation only offers minimal protections when the market is hot, she said. It did not "change the course of change" in Crown Heights North, although advertising the historic nature of the neighborhood might have been one of a number of factors that attracted gentrifiers, she conceded.[44]

The Changing Racial Makeup of Central Brooklyn

Let us take a moment to situate the various observations about demographic change made by the residents of Prospect Heights and Crown Heights North in numerical data. Brooklyn is much less simply Black and White than Baltimore, nevertheless the trajectory of demographic change in Brooklyn can be considered along this axis—either as a change in percent Black or as a change in percent White, each of which indicates something slightly different.

Brooklyn is home to many races, and central Brooklyn has been majority Black since the post-WWII period of White flight, so profound changes in the Black population indicate major neighborhood shifts. All three neighborhoods discussed in this chapter are predominantly Black neighborhoods, and figure 3.2 shows that all three became significantly less Black over the decade for which I have data.[45] Crown Heights North and Prospect Heights went from being approximately 75 percent Black in 2005 to 65 percent Black in 2014, although not in a linear fashion. The Black population of Bed-Stuy declined more profoundly, if again not consistently, from just less than 73 percent to just more than 53 percent.

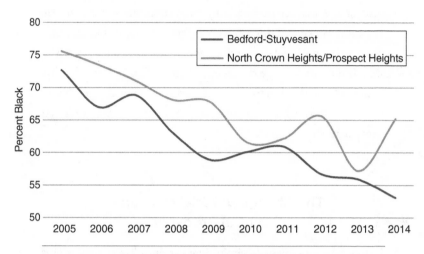

FIGURE 3.2 Black population in central Brooklyn neighborhoods

Source: NYU Furman Center CoreData.nyc

To the degree these have been symbolically Black neighborhoods, Bed-Stuy in particular,[46] radical demographic shifts over a single decade undermine that discursive identity. Bed-Stuy's decline in Black population represents the clearest example of rapid gentrification and displacement when looked at in combination with the data on the White population. In that regard, the 2010–2015 data for North Crown Heights/Prospect Heights (NCH/PH) represent a kind of equilibrium.[47]

The gentrification of these neighborhoods is further evident when we look at demographic change from the inverse perspective, the increase in the White population (figure 3.3). The White population of all three neighborhoods increased significantly, from 2.4 percent in Bed-Stuy and 7.4 percent in the other neighborhoods to 22 percent to 27 percent. This constitutes a 192 percent increase in North Crown Heights/Prospect Heights and a whopping 1,042 percent increase in Bed-Stuy. There is a

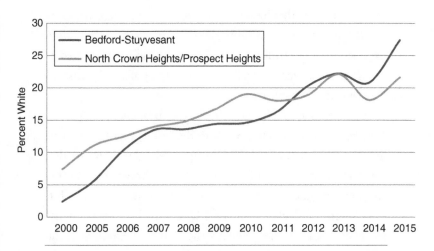

FIGURE 3.3 White population in central Brooklyn neighborhoods

significant, if small to moderate, and relatively stable Hispanic/ Latinx population in all of these neighborhoods, averaging 11.7 percent in North Crown Heights/Prospect Heights and 19 percent in Bed-Stuy throughout the period.

This increase in White residents is important. As Sampson has shown clearly in Chicago, neighborhoods beyond a threshold of approximately 50 percent Black rarely gain White population; instead, they tend to become Blacker. In Sampson's Chicago, as well as elsewhere in the United States, the neighborhoods that make this kind of shift typically experience significant institutional intervention, including the demolition of extensive low-income housing.[48] As Sampson has shown, the kind of neighborhood conversion people worry about when they fear gentrification is extremely rare.

It is striking that we do not see any major institutional intervention in central Brooklyn during this period, certainly not the kind of wholesale demolition and reconstruction of entire public housing projects that Sampson described, even though we do see significant change in neighborhood demographics. Brooklyn's experience of gentrification is distinct and is probably tied to being part of an economically thriving metropolis with a distinct shortage of affordable housing.

The presence of Hispanics/Latinx in Brooklyn, unlike Baltimore, is also important. Some evidence suggests that Whites are less resistant to Hispanics as neighbors, and we can speculate that the larger number of Hispanics in Bed-Stuy may be part of the story of that neighborhood's most rapid increase in White population and decline in Black.[49] Of course, Bed-Stuy was also the poorest and cheapest neighborhood at the beginning of this period, an important factor for in-movement (lower rent) and a risk factor for displacement (lower income households are more likely to face forced moves with changing neighborhood costs of living).

To the degree that these neighborhoods remain overwhelmingly majority-minority, decades from being majority White even if recent trends continue, it is striking that at least one of my interviewees consistently overestimated the White population. Veconi, president of the PHNDC, explained with confidence, citing his own recollection of the Census data, that in 2000 Prospect Heights was 55 percent Black and 33 percent White, but that by 2014 those proportions had more than reversed to 28 percent Black and 58 percent White. Veconi further speculated that neighborhood median household income doubled between 2000 and 2010.[50] My data are at the subborough level, including Crown Heights North, but these data certainly put such a recollection into question. More important than correcting Veconi, however, is reflecting his experience: His version of the neighborhood's trajectory clearly captures a sense of transition.

BEDFORD-STUYVESANT

Bed-Stuy provides an opportunity for me to observe local advocacy for preservation firsthand. Unlike Prospect Heights, whose prominent Prospect Heights Neighborhood Development Council evaluated proposed changes and made landmarking recommendations, Bed-Stuy does not have a single organizational voice for preservation. Instead, an ad hoc landmarks committee of Community Board 3 (CB3) is the volunteer appointed voice of the community and fulfills this purpose by reviewing and recommending to the board itself. This committee includes Morgan Muncey, a local realtor and resident, who brought me with him to the committee's meetings in May and June in 2016.

The Landmarks Committee gathered in the Community Board's offices in Restoration Plaza on Fulton Street, a big commercial strip in Bed-Stuy. Approximately fifteen men and women, evenly divided between Black and White and with slightly more women, gathered around a large table to listen to presentations from local homeowners and their representatives. The meeting was led by two CB3 members, but it actively involved all present. I was introduced to two local residents and preservation advocates who were members of the committee, Reno Dakota and Omar Walker, and I draw primarily on my interviews with them here.

When Reno Dakota, new to Brooklyn from Manhattan and describing himself as "White, gay, [and] atheist," bought a Bedford-Stuyvesant brownstone in 2004, the real estate market was full of flippers and con men, including one who tried to sell Dakota and his partner a house he did not own. Upon settling in Bed-Stuy, Dakota reports that he "automatically felt that we need[ed] to do whatever we need to do to preserve this," referring primarily to the aesthetics of the historic neighborhood.[51]

Part of the neighborhood was already protected by the Stuyvesant Heights landmark district (designated in 1971), but what Dakota calls "Stuyvesant East" was not landmarked.[52]

Dakota learned that CB3 had an ad hoc landmarks committee (overseeing changes in the Stuyvesant Heights district and advocating for new districts) and got involved. Dakota did not get along well with the chair of the committee, describing her as smart and well-meaning but guided by "what God tells me to do" (neither consultative nor transparent) and prone to giving directives. Dakota ultimately rebelled: "You are not Charlie, and we are not your angels!" This outburst pleased some on the committee but permanently offended others. Dakota "considers [him]self the wrong demographic" for Bed-Stuy and recognizes that may have contributed to the conflict.

Dakota identified the key obstacle to a Stuyvesant East district as lack of support from the local city councilperson, whom he describes as "completely uncommunicative." All of the parts of Bed-Stuy that have successfully designated are in the thirty-sixth council district, whose councilperson is involved and supportive. Stuyvesant East is in the fortieth. A councilperson has to bring the proposal for a landmark district to the LPC, and the LPC is unwilling to shortcut that process even when a councilperson is recalcitrant. This may be because landmark districts ultimately require city council approval and are, thus, unlikely to succeed without an official champion to shepherd them through the final vote. Advocates for a Stuyvesant East district have resolved that the only remedy is to wait for this particular councilperson's term to conclude.

Despite this political hurdle, Dakota believes the prospects for landmarking get better every day in terms of community opinion. The neighborhood is becoming more and more conspicuously gentrified, which certainly squares with my observations.

Dakota remarked that as "hideous things are being built along Halsey" his neighbors are coming to believe that "if we don't designate, developers are going to come here, and developers do not care; they don't contribute to preserving the neighborhood." Omar Walker, another member of the CB3 landmark committee, is redoing the top-floor apartment in a Bed-Stuy brownstone his family has owned since 1941 while living in the ground floor himself.[53] He values the local use of landmarking as an opportunity to slow gentrification, but he is also an architect who disagrees with it "fundamentally" because he does not like the constraints landmarking imposes on design. Walker says the community of local homeowners (a mix of newer and older) has taken up preservation specifically in response to what they see has happened on Fulton Street, namely, lots of unrestrained commercial development. Unrestrained construction has been rampant throughout the neighborhood prior to or outside of landmark districts. Locals, therefore, perceive landmarking as an opportunity to prevent unwanted aesthetic changes on their blocks.

Walker is adamant, however, that historic preservation does not preserve community. He argues that people have been "saving homes" in Bed-Stuy for a long time, that it is not just a recent phenomenon. Moreover, and contrary to a common assumption and my characterization of neglect through redlining, he does not think this was just a matter of default: "People say 'poverty preserves,' but people cared about these houses."

Although many in New York City conjure images of inner-city crime when they think of Bed-Stuy, longtime resident Walker has a different view. The neighborhood, he told me, was maintained well throughout the twentieth century, and the community living here was "doing just fine." There used to be more shootings, he admits, but he is more interested in the fact that those occurred without significant police response. There is a noticeably greater police presence in the past two or three years, and he wonders: "Were the people living here before not worth protecting?," or are the police protecting the new people from those who were here already? As a young Black man, Walker particularly objects to "feeling like . . . a criminal in [his] own neighborhood."

All of my central Brooklyn informants perceived landmarking as the primary vehicle available to them to stem the tide of gentrification and the changes to their neighborhood brought by the influx of educated White professionals, but many recognized the limitations of landmarking in this regard. Historic district designation can preserve the physical environment of a historic neighborhood, but it cannot prevent market forces from increasing property prices nor the demographic change that often accompanies those increases. Walker is perhaps clearest about this. Despite these reservations, none can point to alternative political approaches for managing such neighborhood change. A number of my informants also recognize that they are part of this process—roughly half of them are White and moved into this neighborhood early in the transition. Finally, their orientation to preservation is not simply instrumental; they value the details of the historic properties they own and live among.

The Changing Socioeconomic Makeup of Central Brooklyn

Education is often used as a good indicator of class transition in U.S. cities. Data from the Furman Center at NYU reaffirm the accounts we have heard about the changes in who, increasingly, lives in central Brooklyn.

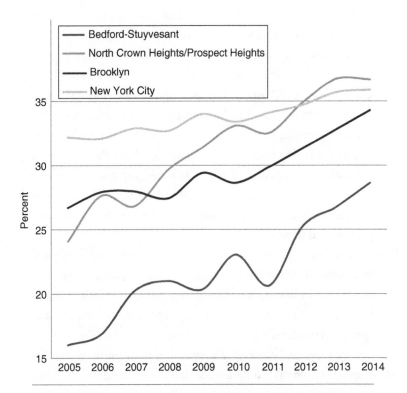

FIGURE 3.4 Percent twenty-five years or older with a bachelor's degree or higher in central Brooklyn neighborhoods and New York City

Source: NYU Furman Center CoreData.nyc

The average percentage of Americans twenty-five years or older with a bachelor's degree or higher rose from 28.4 percent in 2005 to 29.3 percent in 2014.[54] Brooklyn was below the national average in 2005, but educational attainment in the borough increased, particularly after 2010, to above the national average and close to that of the city (figure 3.4). This generally suggests a changing position for Brooklyn in the broader class composition of New York City, one that fits with its gentrification by people who would formerly have lived in Manhattan.

The class transition in the central Brooklyn neighborhoods considered here is conspicuous in terms of education. North Crown Heights/Prospect Heights begins as a slightly below average Brooklyn neighborhood in 2005, changes rapidly in the period right after the Great Recession in 2007, then accelerates again in 2011. The neighborhood winds up above the average for the entire city in 2014, which includes highly professionalized spaces such as the Upper West Side of Manhattan. This indicates a neighborhood increasingly attracting professionals, with professional incomes.

Bed-Stuy's change is roughly as fast but more profound, starting well below the borough, city, and national averages at 16 percent, indicating a neighborhood of service workers, manual and manufacturing labor, trades, and the unemployed and the underemployed. The neighborhood in 2014 is about at the national average, suggesting a rapid influx of professionals. Of course, we cannot differentiate between longtime residents attaining education and better-educated people moving into the neighborhood. However, the fact that the rate of increase in all three central Brooklyn neighborhoods outpaces increases at the borough, city, and national level suggests in-movement and a class transformation of these spaces.

The Trajectory of Housing Prices in Central Brooklyn

Finally, it is worth looking at changes in housing prices in central Brooklyn. These data provide a more direct measure of displacement pressure insofar as housing costs are often the immediate cause of displacement. People frequently leave neighborhoods, or do not select into them, when confronted with rising housing costs. These decisions, in turn, skew demographic shifts toward higher-status populations. This process is not, of course, straightforward or linear. Rising rents result more directly in out-movement than do rising prices for owner-occupied housing because mortgages lock in the cost of owner-occupied housing. Changing rents as a mechanism for displacement in New York City are further complicated by the city's various rent regulations (rent control and rent stabilization), which are intended to maintain affordability. To the degree that homeowners feel pressure due to rising housing prices, it results from increasing property taxes and bills for city services. These fees are most problematic for households living on fixed incomes, especially retirees.[55] At some point, however, increasing home values can function as a positive kind of push factor for homeowners, encouraging them to capitalize on their investment.

Data on house prices are available at the neighborhood level for central Brooklyn and offer a window into the process. Overall, what we see in central Brooklyn are steeply rising housing prices (figure 3.5). To be sure, they fell in response to the mortgage crisis, but they had more than recovered by 2015—increasing threefold from 2000 (a little less in Bed-Stuy, a little more in North Crown Heights/Prospect Heights).

To provide a sense of the pressures on homeowners in the area, we can look at the likely impact of rising house prices on property taxes. Property is assessed annually in New York City, and property tax rates increased from 2000 to 2015 (from 11.6 percent to 19.6 percent for residential properties up to three units, and from 10.8 percent to 13.4 percent, but then back down to 12.9 percent, for larger residential properties).[56] There are exemptions for part of the property value for veterans, but

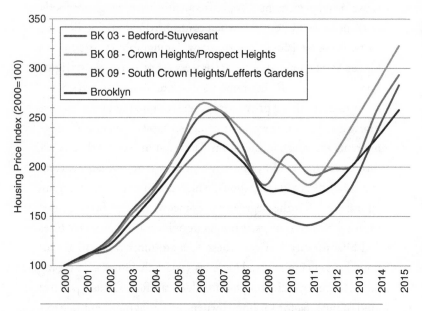

FIGURE 3.5 Index of housing price appreciation, all types, by community district in central Brooklyn, 2000–2015

it is safe to assume that property tax bills more than tripled in the same period that property prices tripled because rates were increasing as assessments were also increasing. To the degree that many residents of central Brooklyn in 2000 were lower-income (a safe assumption for Bed-Stuy given what we saw about college education in the neighborhood), these changes are likely to have created pressure—both negative and positive—to leave.

The rent data at the subborough level reflect similar pressures on renters (figure 3.6). It is notable that rents in these central Brooklyn neighborhoods remain below average for the borough, indicating that these gentrifying neighborhoods are still catching up to Brooklyn Heights, Park Slope, Cobble Hill, etcetera.

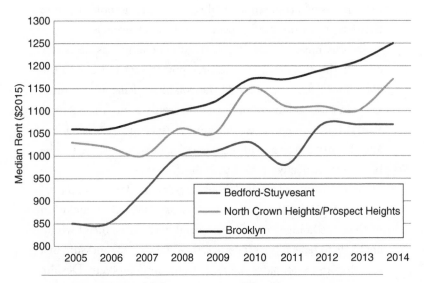

FIGURE 3.6 Median rent in central Brooklyn, 2005–2014

Nevertheless, the change is stark. It is not surprising that the increases are steepest for Bed-Stuy, but the trend for North Crown Heights/Prospect Heights is less clear (some increase, but unstable). This may be a feature of the data, which are only available in the subborough aggregate. Anecdotally there is reason to believe that rents in Prospect Heights are the highest of all the neighborhoods under consideration.

One way of measuring the likely effect of such increases in rent on neighborhood change is to create an affordability measure for each neighborhood. It is simple to calculate such a measure by dividing the median rent by median household income (MHI). Housing experts generally agree that rent should constitute no more than 30 percent of household income. Beyond this point, households confront "shelter poverty," an inability to pay for necessary goods and services because of the fixed cost of rent.

(This is less of a concern for higher-income households because they have more disposable income in absolute terms.)

By this measure, the Brooklyn subborough areas decisively crossed the threshold into shelter poverty around 2009. The volatility in figure 3.7 reflects the volatility of income as measured in these neighborhoods (median rents climb more consistently), but the trend lines indicate a distinct and increasing rent affordability concern. Although volatile, income in these neighborhoods is effectively flat but is much higher in North Crown Heights/Prospect Height (about 14 percent). Medians conceal a great deal, and the income median is distorted by inclusion of all of the homeowners in each neighborhood, some of whom are likely to have higher incomes, thus skewing the measure in a way that underestimates the rent affordability problem. Despite

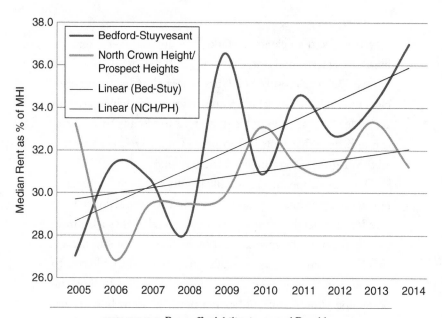

FIGURE 3.7 Rent affordability in central Brooklyn

all of these caveats, this remains clear evidence of direct displacement pressure.[57]

CONCLUSION

In Baltimore I puzzled through a variety of hypotheses about the relationship between historic district designation and neighborhood change, observing a range of neighborhood conditions and periodization. In Brooklyn, neighborhood change was already well underway, and landmark district designation was coming afterward. Rather than asking if one caused the other, in Brooklyn I ask why landmarking is the strategy neighborhood residents chose, how it is facilitated or frustrated by the city government, and how it does or does not mitigate the effects of gentrification.

First, and perhaps most important, landmarking is the primary apparatus available to residents to intervene in a process of gentrification that they perceive is changing their neighborhoods. This is true from the perspectives of both local laypeople and preservation professionals inside and outside government. Furthermore, none of my informants are aware of alternative political approaches to managing gentrification. It is not so much that landmark district designation is the strategy of choice but that it is the only tool available.

Although my informants' concerns were primarily about the demographic change they see affecting their neighborhoods, their orientation to preservation is not simply instrumental, or desperate, but also aesthetic. They are driven to undertake the districting effort because they are admirers of these historic designs and turn to landmarking to defend those designs in extremis. They uniformly recognize the limitations of landmarking: It can preserve the physical environment of a historic neighborhood but cannot prevent an increase in property prices or prevent new kinds of people with new magnitudes of wealth from moving into the neighborhood. Some of my informants also recognize that they are part of this process of neighborhood change, acknowledging that they are racially distinct from the longtime majority of the neighborhood and perhaps implicitly acting to take some responsibility for the undesirable and indirect effects of their own presence.

My Baltimore story was mostly about variation from neighborhood to neighborhood, recognizing the interaction effects of historic district designation as they varied from place to place. But my central Brooklyn story is about commonality across continuous neighborhoods. This commonality inspired the model in figure 3.8.

My reason for introducing this model is to foreground the group-building process my informants described. The prominent

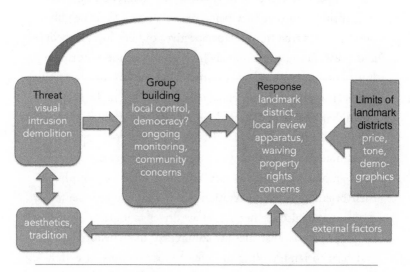

FIGURE 3.8 Conceptual model of landmark districting dynamics

causal connection may be between a perceived threat to the neighborhood and the designation of a landmark district, but the mediating mechanism is a social process of building collective action that, as Bankoff notes, may be at the foundation of the effect landmark districting has on neighborhoods in New York City. This process has repercussions for many other neighborhood concerns—predatory lending, foreclosure, eviction—and points to the possibility that landmark districting is not just the only approach available but is an appropriate response to gentrification.

Taken together, my Baltimore and Brooklyn inquiries clearly show that historic preservation regulation is one of the few policy avenues available to residents to influence change in their neighborhoods. In Baltimore, designation can consolidate status or facilitate changes. In Brooklyn, designation mitigates change. These two examples at either end of a spectrum of development and affordability encourage us to explore other neighborhoods that might further complicate our understanding of historic preservation and neighborhood change.

4

VACANCY, ABANDONMENT, DEMOLITION BY NEGLECT, AND PROJECT CORE IN BALTIMORE

I have examined the relationship between historic district designation and neighborhood change in two very different cities, Baltimore (chapter 2) and central Brooklyn (chapter 3). I emphasized how much the relationship can vary from city to city, even neighborhood to neighborhood, but I also examined historic designation's varying role as a mechanism for urban policy making or community intervention. One purpose for examining Baltimore and Brooklyn was to complicate the presumed relationship between historic preservation and neighborhood change. Finer-grained data like mine reveal that it is not straightforwardly causal, and the direction envisioned by the conventional account may even be backward. But these distinctive cities deserve further investigation with regard to the qualities that make them so different. My task now is to consider preservation's role in one city plagued by vacancy and abandonment (chapter 4) and another subject to intense development pressure (chapter 5).

Baltimore's historic structures and their relationship to neighborhoods present problems specific to legacy cities that have lost a significant proportion of their population and employment base. Population has declined by approximately

36 percent from the middle of the twentieth century to the present day,[1] and many of the homes and workplaces of those nearly 340,000 departed people have been left vacant. The preservation literature is filled with optimistic discourse about "rightsizing,"[2] adjusting the built environment and infrastructure of legacy cities to their current population in the interest of encouraging revitalization. However, the scale of vacancy in Baltimore (and in a number of other cities) is such that the sheer numbers make optimism difficult. As one Baltimore preservationist told me, "trying to do preservation in this huge overwhelming problem is very difficult."[3]

Baltimore has vast numbers of older buildings, historic by definition, that go unused or underused simply by virtue of there being fewer residents to use them. These buildings are effectively abandoned and are threatened by the forces of entropy. In some cases, the buildings have become the property of the city, although the resources necessary to seize them are often unavailable for the same reason the buildings are empty—the city's decline. More often they remain technically the property of an individual or have been foreclosed upon by a bank. The buildings have often been ignored and uninhabited for decades and are subject to fines for their condition and tax arrears. Complications associated with their current ownership are the primary obstacles to the city's ability to seize them. The incomprehension of neighborhood residents about this procedural complexity with regard to places they experience as home leads residents to believe city officials are incompetent and corrupt.

Comprehending the scale of this issue is key to both assessing its impact and addressing it, but the scale proves a challenge in itself. James Cohen explained that one of the key problems associated with unused housing is counting it. In 2001, according to Cohen, the "number of abandoned housing units in [Baltimore was] between 12,700 and 42,480,"[4] an almost ludicrous degree of uncertainty. The measurement problem stems from legitimate concerns such as how long a housing unit must be empty to be considered abandoned, which is compounded by who should do the counting, but the huge range and difficulty of establishing a clear answer points to the scale of the problem and the difficulty in addressing it.

Cohen does four other things in this piece that are important to keep in mind while we dig deeper into these issues.[5] Housing abandonment has often been treated as a symptom of urban decline, and Cohen explains that it also needs to be understood as a cause: "Abandoned homes are symptomatic of other problems, [but] they also contribute to neighborhood decline and frustrate revitalization efforts."

Second, he explores the expense associated with rehabilitating abandoned housing, pointing to the necessity for significant subsidies to make rehabilitated housing affordable to existing residents. In the three neighborhood revitalization plans he examines, subsidies are required to produce affordable units (according to neighborhood median incomes) that range from $36,000 in Historic East Baltimore to $80,000 in Sandtown-Winchester.

Third, and related, Cohen argues that neighborhood housing plans must respond to the needs of existing residents because plans that rely on attracting new, relatively wealthier residents are unrealistic in the context of decades of disinvestment and decline. Beyond housing rehabilitation, this will require significant investment in "employment, economic development, health, public safety, and school-reform initiatives."

This gets to the fourth contribution. All plans for dealing with abandonment need to balance neighborhood input with an overall sense of the city's structure, resources, and trajectory—a standard problem with community planning—to succeed it can neither be exclusively bottom-up nor top-down. A critical comment by Culhane and Hillier, published with Cohen's piece, reaffirms the difficulty of doing anything, pointing to local government fiscal constraint, private investors' uncertainty, and the unlikelihood of significant new federal spending.[6]

Rates of vacancy and abandonment vary widely across Baltimore, and empty buildings are scattered throughout neighborhoods. The people who left the city after 1950 did so for systemic reasons (the postwar suburban boom, racism in lending, etc.), but they left in an unsystematic pattern. This may seem obvious, but the effect is important. Although entire neighborhood populations of residents left, they left gaps throughout existing neighborhoods rather than uniformly vacating areas of the city. The same could be said, of course, of those who have remained—they are distributed among blocks sometimes full of others, sometimes dominated by vacant buildings. Their location is substantially determined by the availability or absence of resources that afford choice in the real estate market. This uneven, inconsistent distribution of vacancy makes the ongoing delivery of city services more complicated and expensive and the consolidation of large tracts of land for new uses more difficult.

PROJECT CORE: SYSTEMATIC DEMOLITION AND BLIGHT REMOVAL

Demolition programs, initiated recently in many legacy cities, attempt to impose some logic on the uneven geography of abandonment. Detroit's program has demolished 20,814 vacant buildings since 2014,[7] completely altering the landscape of the city and dramatically constraining preservation efforts. Project CORE (Creating Opportunities for Renewal and Enterprise) was announced with great fanfare in January 2016 by Maryland Governor Larry Hogan. It was positioned as the state's effort to support Baltimore by addressing the vacancy and abandonment crisis.

Project CORE originally proposed to demolish 4,000 units, or about one-fourth of the 16,000-plus reported abandoned by the city, in four years and support extensive revitalization. CORE intended to introduce new efficiencies into the demolition process by focusing on clearing entire blocks of buildings rather than scattered demolitions on still-inhabited blocks that then require expensive stabilization. This effort would be funded by almost $714 million from the state and implemented primarily through the Maryland Stadium Authority, a government organ with redevelopment experience on a large scale.[8]

Alan Mallach argued initially that legacy cities needed to be rightsized, removing abandoned buildings in a way that the remaining built environment is appropriate to serve the current population.[9] Recent scholarship on demolition is substantially defined by the contrast between Mallach's initial position, widely shared, and that of Jason Hackworth. Hackworth argues that ad hoc demolition in U.S. cities in decline (he does not use the term "legacy cities") has removed more housing than the federally funded urban renewal of the late 1950s through the early 1970s, but that the neighborhoods affected were not improved by this work. Hackworth labels more than 260 neighborhoods in forty-nine U.S. cities as "extreme housing loss neighborhoods," and he argues that they were further damaged by demolition, their marginalization exaggerated.[10] Moreover, Hackworth suggests that race is a key component in the ad hoc process.[11] Mallach's position has shifted over time and become more skeptical, emphasizing the need for a comprehensive strategy that addresses structural factors when attempting to improve the landscape through mass demolition.[12]

Note that the ad hoc programs Hackworth criticizes and Mallach moves away from—roughly demolishing abandoned houses wherever they are found—are different from the purportedly systematic approach to demolition undertaken by CORE, although a systematic approach might still have unequal outcomes. A recent report by the Urban Institute illustrates what Morgan State University professor Lawrence Brown has aptly characterized as the two shapes that describe racialized inequality in Baltimore (figure 4.1): "the Black butterfly" and "the White L."[13]

The Urban Institute report goes on to demonstrate that other measures of inequality such as poverty follow the same butterfly pattern, whereas most of the investment in Baltimore, particularly through real estate sales and lending, is concentrated in the L. Unfortunately, Project CORE uses an analysis of Baltimore housing markets that reflects this same pattern as its guiding mechanism for targeting demolition and rehabilitation funding to encourage revitalization, which likely reinforces this pattern.[14]

The Project CORE quarterly report for fiscal year 2017 explains that "Baltimore City has 297 distinct neighborhoods, of which 120 are in a Stressed Housing Market, based on Baltimore City's 2014 Housing Market Typology. A stressed neighborhood is where 6 percent to 30 percent of the housing stock is vacant."[15] CORE demolition funds are primarily directed to stressed areas, parts of the city already suffering from decades of disinvestment, and most revitalization funds are channeled into middle market and choice areas, parts of the city that have held their value through ongoing investment or that have recently attracted new attention. There is a conspicuous economic efficiency logic here, but it reproduces historical inequality.

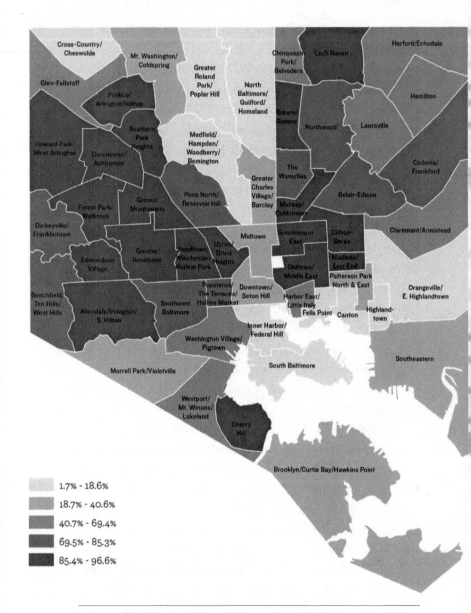

	1.7% - 18.6%
	18.7% - 40.6%
	40.7% - 69.4%
	69.5% - 85.3%
	85.4% - 96.6%

FIGURE 4.1 The Black butterfly and the White L
(percent Black by neighborhood)

Source: Urban Institute, February 5, 2019, https://apps.urban.org/features/baltimore
-investment-flows/.

I rely on a range of sources to construct a profile and critique of Baltimore's ongoing Project CORE. I begin by integrating press coverage, primarily from the *Baltimore Sun*, with the comparative investigation of CORE in a master's thesis on historic preservation by Kacy Rohn.[16] I use Rohn's work primarily for the data she provides, which is hard to come by from Project CORE, but I also take her critique seriously. I put these sources into conversation with interviews with Johns Hopkins, executive director of Baltimore Heritage, and Eric Holcomb, executive director of the Commission on Historic and Architectural Preservation and Historic and Architecture Preservation Division Chief, City of Baltimore, on their role in and perceptions of the project and its underlying process from a preservationist perspective, both from inside the city bureaucracy and advocating from outside it. Finally, I analyze the quarterly reports on the progress of CORE published by the Maryland Department of Housing and Community Development, beginning with the period from April through June of 2017 and extending through the quarter concluding in June 2018.

Profile and Critique

How new and different is Project CORE? Close scrutiny by the press suggests that "just $61.5 million [of the announced $714 million] represents a clear, increased pledge of taxpayer funds that would not otherwise have been available to help rebuild Baltimore over the next four years." These funds were not yet even budgeted at the time of Hogan's announcement and the corresponding *Baltimore Sun* editorial.[17] Rohn concurs, quoting a report by the Maryland Department of Legislative Services:

> Roughly 90 percent of the project's financing was "either already-planned DHCD funding, already-anticipated tax credits, or

subsidized financing that is not appropriate for demolition work and is not direct State support." This analysis also raised numerous questions about whether C.O.R.E. was in fact new programming, rather than a repackaging of existing DHCD efforts.[18]

Rohn also notes that calling the project "Creating Opportunities for Renewal and Enterprise" implies a long-term focus belied by the emphasis on rapid demolition as evidence of progress and the seemingly "haphazard" approach. Demolition clearly "creates opportunities" in clearing vacant properties, but renewal and enterprise are much more complex processes that require the integration of programs, patience, and time. More important, renewal efforts, if they yield anything, often do so over the span of multiple mayoral or gubernatorial terms, thus making them less attractive as investments of political capital because their yields might accrue primarily to one's successor.

Rohn's interviews with preservationists suggest that "opinions are mixed." "They had agreed early on not to oppose the entire project," but hoped that CORE might focus more and more broadly on preserving historic resources.[19] The preservationists Rohn spoke with are affirmatively involved in the process of selecting properties for demolition, but

> despite the veneer of a carefully deliberative process [they] report that the execution process is quite rushed. . . . Sites are selected for expediency, and not in coordination with a larger redevelopment plan. One stakeholder expressed the view that any attempt to match demolitions to a strategy for reuse of the site is "secondary to blight clearance."[20]

My interviewees confirm some aspects of this account and dispute others.

CORE is supposed to involve a significant component of community input in the process of targeting resources, but Rohn reports that the associated outreach efforts are more for show than they are substantive. She refers, for example, to a public demolition meeting on June 29, 2016, soliciting resident input despite the fact that a list of properties to be demolished had been circulated among stakeholders in February and the decision-making process about demolition and stabilization was well underway. This "belies the claim that this is a process driven chiefly by the community's 'wish list' of what should come down." One might not expect residents to favor demolition, although the observation that the vacant properties contribute to crime is common. Rohn reports the sense that disinvestment has been so long-running and intense that "*any* investment is seen as a positive." She quotes a preservationist who calls this "planning from a point of despair" and claims that the choice to support demolition in these circumstances may not really represent a choice at all.[21]

Nineteen months after Project CORE's introduction, Ian Duncan reported that only $5 million of the state's money had been spent and that the Maryland Stadium Authority had demolished 131 houses. Since the project's initiation, the vast majority of demolitions in the city were funded and undertaken by the city itself, most of these because of safety issues associated with collapsing buildings (thus demolitions that would have happened regardless). By late 2017, the advertised goal of the program had shifted to "blight removal," allowing its political boosters to include rehabilitated units as well as demolished ones in the total.[22] The difficulty of claiming title to abandoned properties and relocating the few residents remaining in primarily abandoned blocks has slowed the process. To whatever degree this reflects the inefficiencies of Baltimore's bureaucracy, it also reflects its diligence (not shortcutting complex procedures). Moreover, although I want to foster some skepticism about the city's capacities, it should be noted that many scholars and local activists would *prefer* a program whose successes involve greater investment in rehabilitation than in demolition. Thus the shift to include that investment in CORE's numbers might be seen as a positive sign, not just spin.

Rohn reports that "reactions to this shift in focus are mixed." It has been generally positive among preservationists and community activists where renewal projects have been funded, but it "has caught off-guard some residents who expected to see the widespread clearance of blighted properties that was promised at Project C.O.R.E.'s outset." Rohn quotes then Delegate Antonio Hayes, whose district incorporates much of west Baltimore: "At the community level when you lay out a vision, when you make that type of commitment . . . their expectation is that is going to happen. I wish when the announcement was made, some expectations were more clearly defined."[23]

In announcing the fourth (and most recent) phase of CORE, Governor Hogan and now resigned Mayor Catherine Pugh reframed its immediate purpose. Crime fighting was mentioned in the original announcement in January 2016, but this idea becomes more prominent in late March 2018. According to a press release from the governor's office, "As part of this new phase, over 500 properties that have been designated by Baltimore City as contributing factors to violent crime will be slated for priority demolition by the Maryland Stadium Authority." Hogan refers in his remarks to a "violent crime crisis," then invites Pugh's comments:

> Reducing violence and crime effectively requires addressing the root causes of hopelessness that then inevitably results in

crime. . . . Through Project C.O.R.E. and our partnership with
Governor Hogan and the State, we are able to expedite the demolition of 500 abandoned buildings which provide a haven for
criminal activity in neighborhoods most at risk.[24]

Accordingly, CORE has become a crime control project first,
revitalization second.

Preservationist Perspectives on CORE

My interviews with Johns Hopkins, of Baltimore Heritage, and
Eric Holcomb, of the Commission on Historic and Architectural Preservation (CHAP), generally confirm and develop the
account that emerges from press coverage and Rohn's work.
Unpacking Rohn's suggestion that preservationists feel "mixed"
about CORE, I found that Hopkins and Holcomb identified positive aspects of the project as stemming primarily from
process and the limitations on resources, whereas elements
that could be improved were primarily with regard to orientation or the distribution of funding between demolition and
stabilization.

Holcomb, part of the city bureaucracy responsible for the
project, might be expected to be more positive about the project than a nongovernmental advocate such as Hopkins, although
they are both involved in targeting properties for demolition
and stabilization (there may be more deference on the part of
other stakeholders to Holcomb than to Hopkins). The process is
the part that Holcomb is most positive about. He describes it as
"arduous" and "painful" but also "thoughtful" and "pretty successful." He suggests, moreover, that "CORE has been very positive"
because it has established a kind of annual review: "Every year

we come back with these lists and we review these things and we understand what's been happening out there on the market and on the street—we sort of ground truth what's happening."[25] Hopkins is present in these meetings but has little positive to say about them.

Where Hopkins and Holcomb seem to agree is that the best aspect of Project CORE, from a preservationist perspective, is its relatively minimal impact. Hopkins told me that "little of historic significance is being demolished." Because big buildings cost too much to demolish, no "signature building" has yet been threatened by CORE. In fact, he thinks the impact, even on blight elimination, remains unclear, in part because what gets cleared is "low-hanging fruit" and tends to be "remote," with little effect on the neighborhood around it.[26] Holcomb frames this in the affirmative, recounting that in meetings where stakeholders select properties for demolition and identify those for stabilization, if preservationists request that particular properties be left alone, this request is frequently honored. Of course, Holcomb admits, "the fact is that everybody knows in that room that we have 16,000 vacant buildings and maybe enough money to tear down a thousand."[27]

Both of these preservation-positive aspects derive directly from the limitation of resources and the complication of the process. A deliberate procedure is required to efficiently target funding that can, at best, only be expected to begin to address the vacancy and abandonment problem. Similarly, because the scale of the problem is so great, it is easy to implement the project without significantly interfering with the historic texture of the city. Hopkins warns that the decisions will get more difficult as the project continues—and they both expect the state to continue funding it—and the demolitions will get closer to the historic core of the city.[28]

Holcomb and Hopkins both agree with Rohn that the comparative ease of spending the stabilization money has made it popular. Holcomb would like CORE to be more "nimble" and for the orientation to shift more toward stabilization:

> But there may come a time where we start to say, "well wait a minute, we want more stabilization because we've been tearing down the worst buildings and some of the other buildings may be closer to healthy real estate markets and we can stabilize and hopefully the real estate market will catch up in that neighborhood or expand to that neighborhood and then we got a redevelopment project."

Holcomb admits, though, that accurate forecasting remains the key problem in the face of the toll time takes on buildings ("they're going to start falling over on their own") and a Baltimore population that continues to shrink overall. "Preservation in a shrinking city" is "less the preservation of the actual architecture [and] more preservation of the character of the neighborhood," which means targeting resources carefully. "The last thing we want to do is stabilize a building and turn around five years from now and demolish it."[29] This is why the annual review is so important. There is a constant process of guessing where the real estate market will catch up, one that Holcomb describes as substantially unpredictable, even for experts on the city.

Lipstick on a Pig

Project CORE quarterly reports do not add much beyond a sense of the state's and city's efforts to frame CORE's pace and results as successes in line with expectations. Again, much of this is about reframing a deliberate process rather than incompetence; the project encountered a difficult procedural reality that conflicted with the high hopes for rapid visible results. The adroit pivot from demolition to "blight removal"—thus counting all stabilized or rehabilitated properties as well as those torn down—in the face of the difficulty of actually demolishing vacant housing features prominently, as Ian Duncan and others have indicated.

The reports list numerous substantial awards made to a variety of entities, ranging from nonprofit developers and community development corporations to the Baltimore City Department of Housing and Community Development. In addition, the state's reports repeatedly emphasize all of the additional state and city funding programs brought to bear on the vacancy problem, obscuring the differences between newly committed and repurposed or refocused money. The key concept here is "leveraging," and there is extensive mention throughout of how much investment CORE's intervention is bringing in, reported in large figures again and again. Early quarterly reports often use the word "projected," betraying an optimistic positioning of the whole project.

The earliest quarterly report available (FY17 Q4) includes information that is provided in a processed version as an appendix in subsequent quarterly reports: scanned versions of "Notices to Proceed" (NTP) with the demolition of specific properties from Baltimore HCD to the Maryland Stadium Authority. Later quarterly reports include similar information but group the notices in phases rather than by neighborhood. This is significant because the original NTPs listed neighborhood in addition to street address, making it easy to observe the concentration of demolitions.

The four NTPs together list 148 demolitions in nineteen neighborhoods, but 84 of them are in just four neighborhoods:

Broadway East, Druid Heights, Mondawmin, and Upton (and 94 in five if the ten in Sandtown-Winchester are included). These neighborhoods not only fall within the Black butterfly, northwest and northeast of downtown Baltimore, but many of them are contiguous with one another and with other neighborhoods in which fewer, but some, demolitions took place. Upton, Druid Heights, and Mondawmin radiate out along a northwest trajectory from downtown, and Sandtown-Winchester is just south of them. Broadway East is to the northeast, surrounded by Berea, Oliver, and Middle East in which demolitions also occurred. Including information about neighborhood makes clear just how geographically concentrated the demolitions are.

Tables like table 4.1 appear in the next two quarterly reports, placing a different kind of emphasis on geographic concentration, but they also disappear from later reports. It may be going too far to read much into this, but it reinforces the sense that the state is trying to de-emphasize the neighborhood

TABLE 4.1 NOTICES TO PROCEED (NTP), FY16 QUARTER 4 BLIGHTED PROPERTY LIST, FROM PROJECT CORE

NTP Number	Date NTP issued to MSA	Number of Properties on NTP	Number of Locations on NTP	Number of Properties Removed	Adjusted Total Number of Properties	Adjusted Total Number of Locations
FY16-01	6/30/16	27	5	0	27	5
FY16-02	8/31/16	26	5	0	26	5
FY16-03	9/22/16	42	10	3	39	9
FY16-04	1/18/17	53	9	3	50	8
FY16-05	9/26/17	20	2	0	20	2
5[3]		168	31	6	162	29

Source: "Project C.O.R.E. FY18 Q2 Quarterly Report," Maryland Department of Housing and Community Development, April 1, 2018, 4.

connection. Notice, too, how few of these properties had actually been removed.

Project CORE has yet to significantly change the historic texture of Baltimore, and it has yet to show signs that it will ever do so. This is a result of two factors in particular: the scale of vacancy and the friction associated with the demolition process. As of February 11, 2019, the city estimates that it has approximately 16,800 vacant buildings,[30] and there are reasons to believe that may be a significant underestimate.[31] As abandonment continues in neighborhoods where it is already intense, even demolishing four thousand homes in the near future may only begin to address the problem—*if* demolition is in fact a solution, which remains unresolved.

The original projections clearly did not take process into account, nor did they acknowledge the difficulty of assessing the scope of abandonment in the city. Perversely, but to the surprised satisfaction of preservation advocates and others, the difficulty of demolition has encouraged the redirection of demolition funds toward rehabilitation and other kinds of neighborhood investment. Project CORE may ultimately support the kinds of neighborhood stabilization that demolition by itself would not, despite my skepticism about programs of systematic demolition.

Vacancy, Deterioration, and Demolition by Neglect in Union Square: CHAP Executive Session, August 1, 1990

The current state of the city of Baltimore that led to Project CORE requires further historical exploration, with a focus on neighborhoods and some broader contextualization. To focus on neighborhoods, I examined the 1990 record of a hearing regarding vacancy, deterioration, and demolition by neglect in the Union Square and adjacent Franklin Square neighborhoods. The Commission on Historic and Architectural Preservation (CHAP) invited concerned community members to give their account of the problems their neighborhoods confronted. CHAP also invited a number of city employees responsible for related areas of maintenance and management to listen and respond. The hearing reveals the various concerns and capabilities of neighborhood preservation activists and Baltimore city employees with regard to properties in decline. Then I contextualize both Project CORE and Union Square's struggles using quantitative data on vacancy in historic districts and never-designated neighborhoods, looking for evidence of a relationship between vacancy rates and historic district designation.

Vacancies at the scale of those in Baltimore seem to lead inevitably to abandonment and demolition by neglect.[32] The forces of entropy, if left unchecked, consume buildings over time, a self-evident observation with important consequences for historic designation. If the owners of old buildings in historic districts who would like to use their property for purposes that conflict with historic preservation regulations simply allow their buildings to decay, they can then claim that the buildings should be torn down because they are a safety hazard and too expensive to rehabilitate. This opens new options for redevelopment that would otherwise have been closed to them due to designation. Of course, this process of decay is equally true for buildings for which no one has grand plans, those just left alone because there is no immediate use for them. Intentional and otherwise, neglect threatens the integrity of historic Baltimore neighborhoods.

While reviewing the CHAP files for some of the more prominent historic districts in Baltimore and those recommended to me by CHAP staff as capturing interesting dynamics, I came across the transcript of the CHAP Executive Session from August 10, 1990. The conversation is fascinating, particularly for the way it reveals how residents and neighborhood activists understand abandonment and demolition by neglect and how their understanding conflicts with the way city authorities represent their ability to address these issues. The concerned residents of Union Square also introduce an issue that has not emerged in previous conversations—the possibility of *corruption*. As the transcript reveals, these residents allege that some of the action in the city around abandonment and redevelopment enriches players in the process in unintended ways. City authorities resist this characterization, but do so in terms of their departments or areas of expertise, not necessarily denying that corruption happens elsewhere in the city's relationship with developers.[33]

Another thing to note, and I return to this constantly in this chapter, is that the CHAP chair, in particular, but others as well, speak in terms of Baltimore's inevitable revival and the need to preserve historic neighborhoods for some hypothetical future in which large numbers of people return. There is at least one naysayer in this group, one "realist," who questions this position. Finally, this hearing from thirty years ago demonstrates that vacancy, abandonment, and the problems for neighborhoods radiating out from them have been ongoing issues of significant concern in Baltimore for a long time.

The hearing includes eight CHAP commissioners, three Union Square residents and neighborhood leaders, CHAP staff, mayor's office staff, and other city housing authorities—22 in all. After introductions, the first speaker is Jo Anne Whitely, the "legislative liaison" for the Union Square Association, who has been researching vacancy for Communities Organized to Improve Life, a Baltimore nonprofit. I first discuss the comments of Whitely, Maryellen Cahill (vice president, Union

Square Association), and Ardabella Fox (president, Union Square Association), then I shift to the responses of John Huppert (director of Housing Inspection) and Ron Miles (neighborhood coordinator).

THE CONCERNED COMMUNITY PERSPECTIVE

This hearing helps us integrate the complications of interpersonal interaction, the problem of information asymmetry, and the contrasting commitments of residents and governmental actors into the broader story of vacancy and abandonment considered elsewhere in this chapter, humanizing the processes those data reflect. The residents of Union Square are trying to inhabit and maintain the historic neighborhood they love, and they perceive the city's inaction in the face of the intense abandonment going on around them to be corrupt, incompetent, or both. Their view, emotionally entangled with the love and defense of their homes and from the level of the street, obscures the broader trends of a city facing radical population decline and the accompanying reduction of resources from tax collection. Whether residents have evidence of corruption or not, they are struggling to explain a malign process that seems intentional because of its magnitude and immediacy. In their defense, the chair of CHAP has a view of Baltimore and its trajectory that seems no more realistic.

Joanne Whitely[34] begins by arguing that the city's involvement in state and federally supported redevelopment projects has left it responsible for much of the abandonment in her area, implying complicity or improper conduct with regard to these projects.

> I do have documentation whereby Baltimore City is a participant in the major UDAG's [*sic*] [Urban Development Action Grants] in our area to a degree, which are in default. When Baltimore City

began participating as a co-entity, it created problems because government was, therefore, unable to do what it might have been able to do more effectively, had it remained apart.

Whitely argues that "the preservation movement has been *taken*," meaning that it has been subverted or overwhelmed by the city's redevelopment priorities. She states her belief that CHAP has been acting in good faith to the best of its limited ability. and she states that she is "here in good faith" too. However, Whitely believes it is necessary to have "very uncomfortable conversations" with CHAP about what can be done, including those buildings permitted for rehabilitation by CHAP but left to collapse.

She makes a complicated claim that the city has been stockpiling "tax sale certificates" (a certificate representing the value of taxes owed, the payment of which would purchase the abandoned property) in violation of the Baltimore City Code and that many of these properties, under the "ownership or control [of] the mayor and city council," were allowed to deteriorate to the point of condemnation because CHAP felt "they simply could not take action on" them. Whitely is arguing that the city is acquiring large numbers of buildings illegally, or at least inappropriately, and letting them deteriorate. The implication is that city ownership of these historic buildings has prevented CHAP from pursuing enforcement action against the owner for violations that they would have pursued in other circumstances.

Whitely alleges, moreover, that the city has included properties for acquisition using "block grant funds" that they already own through the tax sale process, implying a kind of double-dealing, and that there "was just too much federal money available," leading city authorities into temptation. Describing the problem with federal funding more generally, she says, "But you see what is happening . . . the federal government relies on the state, the state relies on the city, and then, when the city is a player in the project, everything goes out the window" through some combination of incompetence and corruption.

Later in the conversation, Whitely alleges that small-time owners of vacant housing are pressured to sell by the city, which they do, to unregistered corporations. When the property then is included in a federally funded redevelopment area, the new owner is bought out at a price much higher than was paid to the original, stressed owner (suggesting that the owners of the corporation had insider knowledge of the impending declaration and boundaries of the redevelopment area), the building is left to collapse, and the city is stuck with the bill for its demolition because the assets of the corporation that owned it have been distributed and the owners of the corporation are untraceable. Whitely concludes, "what I am trying to say to you is that the City of Baltimore, the Department of Housing and Community Development has no business getting involved in any transaction with anyone who does not have proper documents."

When asked how she would address the problems she has identified, Whitely responds at length with an emotional appeal:

> I don't know what the answer is. All I know is, that the value of our homes has been impacted. The dream that we had was literally halted when Urban Renewal came to be . . . and we were told that Urban Renewal and Preservation could co-exist. . . . What I am trying to do is appeal to you as a governmental body and also from a more humanitarian standpoint. We came in [to homeownership in Union Square] and we had a dream and our dream became threatened when the wheeling and dealing began almost like insider trading. . . . I am begging you to help us retrace what happened and to see to it that no other neighborhood goes through it,

and to ask the City to immediately stabilize the properties in our historic district and there are a number of them.

Whitely's complaints echo standard complaints about dealing with government bureaucracies and question whose interests are served by government action. They also point to a cultural-structural-institutional gap that is central to many of the concerns voiced here and by preservation activists elsewhere in my research. For residents, historic buildings are foremost home and neighborhood—sources of pride, identity, senses of safety and security. For CHAP and for Housing and Community Development, they are properties to be managed according to regulations and relying on scarce resources. Everyone in this particular story could be blameless and in the right, fulfilling their positional responsibilities appropriately, and still be far apart in their understanding of the situation because of the differences of their orientation to the built environment that derive from their position in the process.

Maryellen Cahill, vice-president of the Union Square Association, continues in a similar vein, emphasizing neighborhood resident experience and its frustrations.

> I am . . . extremely involved in my neighborhood and hope to become more involved in Baltimore City. The amount of time that it takes to get anything resolved in regards to a vacant building in our area or in any area in the City, is absolutely outrageous. . . . there are many people out there like me. They want to do something and they have had it. They are fed up. They're fed up with all these boarded up buildings. They're fed up with absentee landlords living out in the county, who could care less about their back yard filled with trash. There is no reason, we feel, that this can't change.[35]

Cahill's primary complaint is about the failure of code enforcement and the difficulty of getting the city to act. She describes countless phone calls, six appearances in court regarding a single deteriorating house, and the perceived insult of $75 fines being imposed, then deferred six months, and only raised upon a return to court.

Cahill echoes Whitely, implying that some corrupt influence is revealed by the difficulty of transferring vacant properties to developers who want to do something with them. At the invitation of CHAP Chair Goodman, they both couch this particular frustration in terms of the potential for growth in Union Square. Whitely cites recent high house prices to demonstrate the neighborhood's success, and Cahill and Whitely both warn that vacancy, abandonment, and empty lots threaten these prices, as does the difficulty of getting the city to address them.

Last among the community representatives is Ardabella Fox,[36] president of the Union Square Association, who complains about "extensive deterioration" in Union Square "caused by neglect, lack of code enforcement." More important, she questions the mechanisms for city intervention and strategies for preserving vacant properties. First she asks, "Why not stabilize?" She has been told that stabilization costs $25,000 per property and demolition costs $15,000, what she calls a "minor difference." She then raises the lien[37] process and asks why "that's where it stops," why the city does "not go further to try to collect this thing?"[38] Cahill also accuses the Department of Housing of allowing the buildings to reach that point of deterioration because "the codes were not enforced on those properties."[39]

Whitely, Cahill, and Fox are insinuating that the city does not care about Union Square and can only be troubled to intervene where federal funding produces an opportunity to profit. I would guess that there is an undertone of racial discrimination—between a predominantly white city administration and an increasingly Black historic district—but the identities of the key players are hard to confirm with only their names at this temporal remove. Cahill's "Why not stabilize?" captures the range of their comments well; there is a simple solution available to the city that would better serve the interests of the neighborhood if only the city were not either too incompetent or corrupt to implement it. As you will see, city authorities claim that this idea is emblematic of residents' misunderstanding of the situation and the city's capabilities.

THE CITY RESPONDS: HUPPERT AND MILES ON ENFORCEMENT AND FEDERAL FUNDING

When the director of Housing Inspection, John Huppert,[40] presents his perspective, he first identifies himself as a longtime Baltimore resident, homeowner, and city worker, sympathetic to their concerns (another positional complication). He also clarifies his responsibility exclusively for code enforcement, "I can't address all the issues that [you] have raised . . . I have nothing to do with UDAGs, HODAGs, CDBG monies, acquisition, disposition, or development." Huppert walks the line between explanation and condescension as he describes the limits of the city's enforcement powers and the scarcity of its resources. He also quickly defines a position that contradicts a number of comments by CHAP Chair Goodman about the city's size and trajectory.

Huppert begins by taking up a fundamental background issue obscured by many of the previous comments: Baltimore's radical decline in population. This also, of course, emphasizes the difference between the neighborhood resident's view from the ground and the city administrator's requirement for a broader, more abstract consideration.

> I think the vacant house problem is substantially more complex
> than anyone here has given it credit for being. The biggest prob-
> lem the City is confronted with is the loss of population . . . peo-
> ple have left the city . . . there are less people here. There is less
> need for housing and that is one of the biggest issues that we're
> going to have to address . . . what do you do with the housing, if
> there's no one to occupy it?

Huppert goes on to discuss the complex question of city ownership of vacant and abandoned housing. He explains that the
city no longer "automatically take[s] title to a building once it
goes to tax sale," meaning that it has reduced its ownership of
vacant buildings from about 50 percent fifteen years ago to about
10 percent in 1990. The previous policy produced a perverse incentive for "irresponsible investors" to buy marginal properties and
milk as much value out of them as possible while allowing them
to deteriorate, then abandon them and leave the city responsible
(for cleaning, sealing, stabilizing, selling). He explains,

> The City has a position now where we don't want to own them.
> We want to force the owners of them to maintain them, to pay the
> taxes, to pay the other costs associated with maintaining them and
> we're interested in pursuing very vigorously in court cases where
> we believe we can have a positive impact. . . . We have to begin
> with the ones where we can be successful.

Now, Huppert says, the city "own[s] a large number of *tax sale
certificates*, but all that means is that no one else bid on the property" (emphasis added).

People can acquire properties for which the city holds the
tax sale certificate ("Every year the city has a tax sale"), but the
city does not technically own them and cannot simply dispose

of them by fiat. He agrees with Cahill, moreover, that there are frequently significant liens against these properties but that the last known address of the owner of the lien is often the abandoned house itself: "You can't find them; they're gone." Huppert concedes to Whitely that some of these properties for which the city holds the tax certificate may also be incorporated into urban renewal plans, as she alleges, and are not available to purchase, but he is "not in a position to discuss that, because I don't know."

Huppert and CHAP Commissioner David Norman explain how liens work. Norman begins by pointing out that it is only possible to collect the value of a lien if the property is sold to a private individual, not if it is transferred to the city government. Huppert goes on to say that the city can pursue "in personam" suits against property owners with large outstanding liens, but they only do so when the value of the lien significantly exceeds the legal costs associated with the suit and when they are convinced that the assets of the property owner are such that the owner might reasonably be compelled to pay off the lien: "There are individuals and corporations, who have absolutely no assets [as alleged by Whitely], and so they are not worth pursuing. But there are individuals who are worth pursuing, and the City Solicitor's Office pursues them vigorously, and does collect money." This, and further related comments, fails to satisfy community members, who feel there ought to be a better way for the city to collect the costs from property owners.

In response to a comment from Cahill, Huppert also distinguishes between property liens and Housing Court fines, for which nonpayment results in arrest. He explains that judges suspend most of the fines and states that these are not a significant source of revenue for the city despite the frequency of penalizable housing offenses. He explains that liens are initiated by many departments in city government, not just Housing, but that they then become the responsibility of the city Solicitor's

Office and are no longer dealt with by Housing or the initiating departments, with the exception of some research on a property owner's assets in particular cases.

Returning to Cahill's "Why not stabilize?," Huppert explains the complications of stabilization, often including significant reconstruction, and he argues that buildings in Union Square will cost many times more to stabilize than to demolish. Cahill accuses the "Department of Housing" of allowing the buildings to reach that point of deterioration because "the codes were not enforced on those properties."[41] Huppert responds:[42]

> I've got 6,000 vacant buildings in the City, and we take three to four hundred of them a year into Housing Court, because that's all the resources that we have. Now, when we get them in, in many instances as you mentioned, we had them in five, six, seven times and the bottom line is a $50–$100 fine, that's not correcting the problem.

Huppert makes another point about shepherding scarce resources and the costs of building stabilization that the city chooses to undertake. I quote him at length.

> Now there was one question that was raised about, why the City is stabilizing privately owned vacant houses in the community when there are City-owned houses in the community? . . . What we look at . . . is stabilizing properties where we can get our money back. . . . We only have the resources to do 200 properties per year and we select properties where the value of the property is substantially greater than the value of the stabilization. . . . The owner [buyer] is going to pay it as soon as we put the property up at the tax sale, because they're not going to want to lose a forty or fifty thousand dollar house because of ten thousand dollars in liens. . . . We have to get our money back from a collection of these liens.

"Code enforcement is not the solution. It is not going to end that problem and bring about the desired result that you're looking for. Not in and of itself."

Other strategies are as yet underutilized, according to Huppert, such as a violation in the CHAP Ordinance called "Demolition by Neglect."

> The only advantage [of pursuing a Demolition by Neglect charge] as opposed to going under the Building Code, is that you can get *a jail sentence.* [qualifies that there are many complications associated with the effort] But we are interested in pursuing that in a selective case. We'd like to find a bad individual, somebody who has a lot of vacant houses, somebody who has big problems all over the City and who also has a vacant house in a CHAP area and on that one, we'll prosecute them on "Demolition by Neglect." I'd like to see an owner of a vacant building put in jail. I'd love it. Because it sends out a clear message. (emphasis added)

"Every sin in this city is not directly attribute[able] to vacant buildings," says Huppert in response to Cahill's allegation implying racial discrimination: "there are some areas, though, that get better attention than other areas."[43] Without addressing the implications of Cahill's allegation, Huppert[44] explains that this pattern is about "cost allocation" above all and needing to use discretion about where to apply scarce resources—the same logic that drives Project CORE decades later. This avoids the question of which kinds of neighborhoods are likely to yield the property values that facilitate returns to the city as it allocates its resources, and the racist and systemic causes for those differences. To further explain the difficulty of enforcement, he says that he has witnessed a radical (two-thirds) reduction in the number of inspectors, even though their responsibilities have increased (33 inspectors in 1987 for 238,000 parcels). This despite the fact that

> Mayor Schmoke held Housing Inspection harmless in the wors[t] budget year that this city has ever had in the twenty years that I've worked for the City. This department [Housing and Community Development] lost fifty bodies . . . and the Mayor said that none of them are to come out of Housing Inspection, and they didn't.

Huppert has portrayed the city's resource situation and the procedures available to it as a correction to complaints from Union Square residents who misunderstand what the city is capable of, however otherwise sympathetic or reasonable they are. Moreover, Huppert contextualizes the city's limited ability to manage vacancy, abandonment, and demolition by neglect in the radical shrinking of its population, which both creates the problem of redundant structures and undermines its resource base. His comments focus on his department and what little it can do, but he actively avoids talking about other elements of the city bureaucracy and the use of federal money, leaving allegations of corruption and self-dealing, for the most part, unaddressed.

Ron Miles,[45] neighborhood coordinator, explains that different parts of the city fall under the responsibility of the District Planner (non-urban-renewal areas that he also describes as "outer city neighborhoods") and the HCD Planner (urban renewal areas). "The District Planner works with Union Square primarily, and in Franklin Square just across the border, which is an Urban Renewal area we have the HCD Planner." He also explains that most of the Community Development Block Grant (CDBG)[46] money is spent in the urban renewal areas.

In response to various questions, comments, and allegations from the community members present, Miles goes on to explain how CDBG money is spent to acquire properties.

In the case of Franklin Square, again they have a Planning Committee within the neighborhood and with a certain allocation annually the neighborhood identifies properties that should be acquired, lots to be developed and many other things, as far as, community development in the neighborhood. In our non-Block Grant areas . . . we're not acquiring properties. [in response to "fishy"] . . . we would plan to acquire the property probably even before it went to tax sale. As we identify properties in a tax sale, I then use the Block Grant money to go through tax sale foreclosure. That way we reduce the time frame that is necessary [for acquisition through CDBG funding].[47]

Miles describes the city's eagerness to transfer tax sale properties to developers but suggests that a basic standard must be met: "We are still open to both non-profit, as well as, private developers in assisting them in acquiring these properties, *if in fact, they can get the rest of the financing that is going to be necessary to develop the site*" (emphasis added). The implication is that this can be quite difficult because these properties are unlikely to yield a profit when redeveloped. References to failed redevelopment efforts at various scales are cited throughout the hearing. City authorities suggest that these were unrealistic projects, whereas community members imply mismanagement or wrongdoing.

This necessity to identify sources to completely fund projects explains another resident concern. Cahill had claimed that nonprofits acquire state funding for projects on the basis of plans to redevelop in a particular neighborhood but then shift the location of their investment, alleging a bait and switch, tricking the funders. Miles responds, "If they don't get complete financing for that project the organizations then go back and reapply to the State to redirect the money," making clear this is neither nefarious nor mismanagement, although it may reinforce the tendency to distribute resources unevenly that Cahill identified earlier.

According to Miles, all of these funding issues and areas for redevelopment are discussed at "the housing roundtable, where all the housing development non-profits get together on a monthly basis." Neither CHAP commissioners nor residents appear to have been aware that such a thing existed.

COMMISSIONERS GOODMAN AND NORMAN AND THE LIMITATIONS OF THE GROWTH PARADIGM

CHAP Chair Deborah Goodman[48] presumes that Baltimore will return to a growth trajectory, and her vision of preservation and neighborhood stabilization is, in part, in service to that. Early in the hearing, in the midst of Joanne Whitely's testimony, Goodman stated the following:

> In the long range view, where the City will go, I think that we have to stem this kind of decay, because it is a matter of time. Certain things will become essential to the City again, and right now you [in historic Union Square] are caught in the middle. You're like in no man's land. You're not attractive for people to move to and yet in the next 20 years the growth will probably go that way, if you can keep these things intact, and I hope that we can do that.

Later in the hearing, Goodman gives an example of the kind of growth she is imagining, driven by the development of a medical center at the University of Maryland in Baltimore.

> I'm trying to think of alternatives to these blocks of houses, in an area like Union Square for instance, which is right on the heel of the University of Maryland. Very valuable strategically for that

school, and with those schools growing as they are, we will probably become a medical center in the next century of research, and so forth.

She goes on to advocate that the city invest in rental housing for students associated with the university, a suggestion immediately derided by Norman. In fact, there is a lot of back and forth between Chair Goodman and Vice Chair Norman; virtually every time Goodman asserts something or takes a position, Norman jumps in to contradict or correct her before anyone else has the chance ("mansplaining," perhaps).[49] This suggests some tension within the commission, compounded, perhaps, by sexist resistance to a woman in a leadership position.

This tension is best illustrated by an exchange in which, again, Goodman assumes a return to growth in Baltimore and Norman expands his argument against her claims based on his understanding of the limited capacity of the city bureaucracy.

> MRS. GOODMAN: See, this is the overall problem that is bigger than the money and bigger than the Block Grant and bigger than the historic district is that matter of no plan. No long range view, because ten years from now when there is . . . because there is no plan and suddenly money would be available, there is nobody to put anything into place and we're all going to pay for this.
> DAVID NORMAN: Debbie, you can't have a plan without an Urban Renewal District being designated.
> MRS. GOODMAN: I'm not sure of that.
> DAVID NORMAN: I'm sure about it. [Norman's position is confirmed by others.]. . .
> MRS. GOODMAN: [in response to explanation of CDBG funds being reallocated from various neighborhoods into a new project and committed for multiple years into the future] So, there

it is. You rob Peter to pay Paul, and end up with your pockets
hanging out anyway.

DAVID NORMAN: But you can't . . . one thing Union Square might
want to consider is petitioning City Council for designation
as an Urban Renewal District. It will get more attention. Now
I happen to be familiar with this process, going through it in
Little Italy when Little Italy did not want to become an Urban
Renewal District. . . . Because to the neighbors of Little Italy,
Urban Renewal means bulldozed down [reference to earlier
era]. . . . A lot of people are afraid of that term. But without
Urban Renewal designation you cannot get money.[50]

We see here the complications of interpersonal interaction, the
problem of information asymmetry, and the contrasting commitments of residents and governmental actors and the relevance of those in the broader story of vacancy and abandonment.

The residents of Union Square have a set of concerns and
a set of expectations that are not in direct conflict with those
of city authorities. Rather, they fit awkwardly: City authorities
have to select carefully among possible interventions because of
their scarce resources, do not experience the vacancy of properties as emotionally immediate, and know the limitations of the
enforcement mechanisms they have at their disposal.

Moreover, disagreement about whether to understand Baltimore as permanently smaller than it once was or in a temporary
population downturn, followed inevitably by a return to growth,
permeates the conversation. Union Square residents seem to
imagine that their neighborhood would grow if vacant properties were easier to acquire. But Chair Goodman seems to understand part of the purpose of historic preservation to be keeping
neighborhood texture in place until it is needed again in the
near future.[51] Only Director of Housing Inspection Huppert is

clear that Baltimore is contending with the problem of extensive housing for which there will never again be a demand. It has been nearly thirty years since that hearing, and we now know that Huppert was the closest to being correct.

This asymmetry is informational but also importantly *positional*. The distinct locations of the contrasting groups of players with regard to processes of abandonment and its management instill interests that are hard to reconcile. City bureaucrats struggle even among themselves to square a growth mission with observations of the reality of Baltimore in this period. Local residents struggle to understand why the city does so little to help them and fall back on racism and corruption as explanations, both of which may well be present but neither of which is sufficient to account for the full dimensions of the situation, even in combination. These conflicts and confusions appear inevitable in the absence of resources that defines the shrinking city context.

VACANCY IN BALTIMORE NEIGHBORHOOD STATISTICAL AREAS

We can place historical demolition by neglect in Union Square and the more recent Project CORE in broader context by returning to the neighborhood statistical area data that I relied on in chapter 2. These data reveal change over time and the city as a whole but also allow us to refocus on designated historic districts (HDs) and their contrast with the rest of the city. On average, Baltimore historic districts, particularly those designated in the earliest cluster, have higher status populations than never-designated neighborhoods, at least as measured by household income, education, and race. Running against the status trend, the average percentage of vacant units in HDs is substantially

TABLE 4.2 AVERAGE VACANCY RATES IN HISTORIC DISTRICTS AND NEVER-DESIGNATED NEIGHBORHOODS

	% Vacant 1970	% Vacant 1980	% Vacant 1990	% Vacant 2000	% Vacant 2010
Historic Districts	2.5	9.9	10.5	15.5	17.5
Never-Designated Neighborhoods	1.4	5.7	6.7	12.3	14.2

higher than that in never-designated neighborhoods, although they converge somewhat over the period (table 4.2).

How residential vacancy rates are connected to the social status of a neighborhood population is not obvious. Higher income should protect households from foreclosure, one of the causes of abandonment. To the degree that income and education are correlated, greater educational attainment might do the same. Whiteness, on the other hand, in a Baltimore that has lost many of its white residents since its population peak might seem likely to increase vacancy over time—we might expect to see more departures from predominantly white city neighborhoods. We might also expect to see more departures from neighborhoods in which the residents had the wherewithal to move, that is, higher incomes ones. All of these are indirect relations that rely on intermediary mechanisms to explain the connection. At the same time, the connection running in the opposite direction is quite clear and direct: Significant vacancy and abandonment damage the status of a neighborhood and the robustness of many neighborhood processes.

Despite the complex connection of vacancy to neighborhood status, vacancy bears obvious relevance for questions of neighborhood change. Vacancy indirectly indicates something about the real estate market; that is, it should, in general, correlate negatively with demand. But vacancy is also relevant for concerns about displacement because it tells us something about how much pressure to move out new in-movers might cause. Finally, vacancy is the logical endpoint of the process of rent capture prior to neighborhood revitalization that is key to at least one prominent theory of gentrification—landlords allowing their properties to decline in anticipation of large-scale neighborhood upgrading creating a rent gap.[52]

Vacancy rates increased greatly in Baltimore over the period for which I have data (figure 4.2). They seem to vary independently of status measures for HD clusters, at least higher status does not seem to consistently predict lower vacancy, although it may increase stability (notable in the vacancy rate of the highest

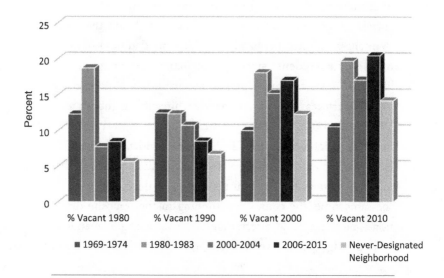

FIGURE 4.2 Housing vacancy by decade in historic district clusters

Data for 1970 is available only for census tracts and not for neighborhood statistical areas and appears to understate vacancy rates.

status, early cluster). In the two earliest clusters (1969–1974 and 1980–1983), vacancy rates prior to designation were much higher than rates citywide, two and half to three times higher. In the 1980–1983 cluster, they remain high, relative to the rest of the city, but in the 1969–1974 cluster they actually decline, in both absolute and relative terms.

In the later clusters (2000–2004 and 2006–2015), vacancy rates prior to designation are much closer to those in never-designated parts of the city and follow a similar trajectory, increasing gradually, but remaining similar to if slightly higher than those in the rest of the city, reiterating the sense that emerged earlier that more recent HDs are more like the rest of the city. The decline in vacancy rates in the earliest HD cluster again suggests the possibility that designation *does something*, but it leaves open the question of why it would do so in one group of HDs but not in the others (except to the degree that historic designation in these neighborhoods captures aspects of privilege that are relevant to stability).

There are lots of interesting negative correlations in the weak to moderate range (–0.31 and –0.55) between vacancy and status variables. Most interesting among the correlations with vacancy rates is the suggestion that lower neighborhood MHI predicts increased vacancy in the future (table 4.3). The negative value of the correlation coefficient for the relationship between MHI and vacancy increases for vacancy rates decades after the MHI observation. This seems plausible if we understand vacancy as, in part, the result of the inability to afford occupancy. Units are abandoned by residents who can no longer afford to live in them, whereas higher household incomes ensure more residential stability and less abandonment. The time lag between decreased income and increased vacancy may reflect the time required for eviction or foreclosure.

TABLE 4.3 CORRELATION COEFFICIENTS FOR MEDIAN
HOUSEHOLD INCOME (MHI) AND % VACANT BY DECADE*

	MHI 1980	MHI 1990	MHI 2000	MHI 2010
% Vacant 1980	−0.37	−0.24	−0.27	−0.19
% Vacant 1990	−0.4	−0.33	−0.28	−0.17
% Vacant 2000	−0.55	−0.46	−0.44	−0.36
% Vacant 2010	−0.53	−0.43	−0.41	−0.35

*All coefficients reported are significant at the highest level.

TABLE 4.4 CORRELATION COEFFICIENTS FOR BACHELOR
DEGREE OR GREATER (BA+) AND % VACANT BY DECADE*

	% BA+ 1990	% BA+ 2000	% BA+ 2010
% Vacant 2000	−0.32274	−0.33238	−0.28681
% Vacant 2010	−0.40392	−0.35831	−0.29839

*All coefficients reported are significant at the highest level.

The associations between vacancy and education are weaker,
but they run in the same direction (table 4.4). In other words,
more better educated people in a neighborhood in one year predicts somewhat lower rates of vacancy in that neighborhood ten
years later and even more twenty years later (these coefficients
are highly significant).

Neighborhood education level in 1980 shows minimal association with vacancy in any year. I suspect this is primarily because
education levels were much lower in the earlier years. Relationships running in the other direction (from vacancy toward education level in the future) are mostly not significant.

Only two correlations between neighborhood percent white
and vacancy rates clear my threshold for a weak association

(R>0.3), and those suggest that whiteness early in the period predicts decreased vacancy in 2010: percentWH80 x percent-Vac10, -0.32; percentWH90 x percentVac10, -0.31. The remaining associations in both temporal directions are too weak to mention, insignificant, or both. These correlations, although weak, run counter to my earlier suggestion that we might expect to see greater rates of vacancy in whiter neighborhoods because of the disproportionate departure of whites from Baltimore relative to Blacks, but the relationships among whiteness and neighborhood advantage should increase.

Returning to my experiment pairing HDs and never-designated neighborhoods that are demographically similar at baseline, then tracking their trajectories across the designation of some, yields some further insight. For the HDs designated in the early 1980s, the protective effect of either extreme whiteness or radically outlying educational attainment stands out in regard to future vacancy. Highly educated HDs Charles Village and Abell outperform smaller, never-designated Kernewood in terms of moderate increases in vacancy, but not never-designated Cheswolde, which also begins and remains much whiter than the other three. Similarly, overwhelmingly white, but poorly educated HD Canton sees moderate increases in vacancy relative to never-designated Brooklyn and Mill Hill, which lost much more of their white population. Canton's vacancy increases are much more like never-designated Morrell Park, which also maintained its white population. The least and less white HDs have much higher rates of vacancy than their pairs and mostly greater increases.

The same seems to be true for the HDs designated in the early 2000s. High white, high educational attainment HDs (thus doubly protected) are similar to their never-designated pairs in moderate baseline vacancy and in increases in vacancy.

High white, low educational attainment HDs (less, but still, protected) have relatively higher rates of vacancy than their pairs, but increase similarly moderately.

To summarize, HDs tend to have higher rates of vacancy than never-designated parts of the city, both before and after designation, although the ways designation and status interact seem to moderate increases in vacancy or protect HDs from it. In the highest status HDs, the earliest cluster, vacancy declined over time in both absolute terms and relative to never-designated parts of the city. In the lowest status HDs, the second cluster, vacancy remains high relative to the rest of the city, and in the latest two clusters, vacancy is much like the rest of the city. Put another way, I cannot detect any consistent correlation between vacancy and historic designation, but lower average status in a neighborhood (defined in terms of income, education, and race) is weakly correlated with higher rates of vacancy in the future whether or not the neighborhood is designated. The causes of vacancy, as current scholarship indicates, are more complex than the age of the structures or the status of neighborhood residents.

CONCLUSION

At its core, the project of this book is to complicate our understanding of the relationship between historic district designation and neighborhood change. Key to that project is noticing that the effects of designation on other neighborhood characteristics is related, among many other things, to cities' growth trajectories. Just as an examination of a rapidly growing Brooklyn is essential, so is one of a shrunken and shrinking Baltimore in which the particularities of vacancy, abandonment, and demolition by neglect constitute the conditions in which historic designation plays its role.

We have seen that rates of vacancy are substantially higher, on average, in designated historic districts in Baltimore than in the rest of the city, both before and after designation. Vacant and abandoned homes create quality-of-life issues that may depress neighborhood status in important ways and function as the mediating factor that explains correlations between vacancy and lower income and less education. Causal explanations that go beyond speculation will require future research, but the 1990 residents of Union Square articulate this assault on their quality of life and cannot understand why the city will not do more to help them remedy it. Various scholars have noticed the unevenness of decline and abandonment, but these are just some of the asymmetries experienced by residents whose relationship to their neighborhood is fundamentally different from that of the city officials responsible for their maintenance, no matter how well intended.

Baltimore's effort to address abandonment, Project CORE, has not produced conspicuous results in terms of its stated goal of demolishing empty housing, nor has it yet affected historic structures profoundly. Somewhat perversely, however, it may be doing something more like what Union Square residents almost thirty years ago were asking the city for—investment in rehabilitation. More time is needed to see what Project CORE becomes and whether any of its effects are important, but the prospect is intriguing. We can say that the relationship between designation and neighborhood change is distinct in the context of shrinkage.[53]

5

STRUGGLING TO PRESERVE IN THE CONTEXT OF AGGRESSIVE DEVELOPMENT PRESSURE

The deeper story about preservation and neighborhoods in Baltimore is about managing vacancy, abandonment, and demolition, as we have seen. It is mostly a top-down story about citywide officials and nonprofits. In central Brooklyn, the deeper story is entirely different. Working to preserve the historic physical and architectural texture of neighborhoods in Brooklyn is the only strategy available to locals who want to maintain the *social* texture against the onrushing tide of development in an expensive city with a steadily intensifying shortage of affordable housing (thus bottom-up). The pressure on the historic neighborhoods of Prospect Heights, Crown Heights North and South, and Bedford-Stuyvesant comes not from radical population decline and the bulldozer but from increasing population pressure and the sometimes devious mechanisms of speculative development.

Community preservationists working in neighborhoods throughout central Brooklyn demonstrate the opportunity that landmarking offers for local residents to resist neighborhood change in the face of intense development pressure. In particular, landmarking provides a process through which development decisions are exposed to public consideration in ways that can bring communities together to address issues beyond the preservation of structures. By and large, in these struggles, local residents' dominant interest is to maintain existing residents in place.

In Bedford-Stuyvesant, where rapid gentrification is underway, neighborhood activists strive to apply preservation regulation to mitigate change but frequently encounter its significant limitations in the face of aggressive development pressures. The Community Board 3 Landmarks Committee[1] is where the intricate business of managing a historically designated neighborhood begins. It is where locals bring violations to the attention of the community and homeowners and where developers request permission for alterations to buildings that contribute to landmark districts. The landmark committees of the Prospect Heights Neighborhood Development Council (PHNDC) and the Crown Heights North Association (CHNA) play the same role. The alterations proposed range from new doors and windows to wholesale remodels that add elevators and rooftop hot tubs. Local boards wield significant power over design decisions, but their power to prevent gentrification is limited. They can insist that speculators maintain the original roofline of a Bed-Stuy brownstone, but they cannot prevent them from renting renovated townhouses for $7,495 to $15,585 per month.[2]

The dynamics are similar in Crown Heights South, where the struggle to designate a neighborhood as historic leads to frustrations as real estate prices skyrocket, longtime residents sell, and renters are displaced. Evelyn Tully Costa, a white homeowner with training in design and preservation, has been working for years to landmark Crown Heights South, but she has been unable to persuade enough of her neighbors of the benefits to gain the attention of the Landmarks Preservation Commission (LPC). Her efforts have also faced resistance from Lubavitcher Hasidic Jewish households nearby that want to be able to expand historic houses to accommodate large families. So she confronts the further challenge of designing a district that does not include this part of the neighborhood. At the same time, the city and state have initiated redevelopment of the historic Bedford Union Armory, which she fears will be undertaken in ways that accelerate gentrification of the neighborhood and undermine a key element of its historic fabric.

The stories in this chapter illustrate how the larger struggle over housing and profit in an expensive city with a shortage of affordable housing often play out at the local level of city government. The frictions inherent in these local processes and the complicated (frequently personality-driven) relationships between individuals and organizations underlie this process. A single individual sometimes effectively constitutes the voice and motive force of an organization, which comes with a particular set of limitations. Community organizations are forced to rely on the social, economic, political, and professional capital of their often volunteer members, and this, too, has risks. Finally, these stories are about specific historic neighborhoods with specific built environments that constrain and inflect the efforts themselves.

I begin by framing these complex neighborhood processes through interviews with two active community-level preservationists, Rob Witherwax and Ethel Tyus. Witherwax is a practicing attorney specializing in real estate transactions, chair of the PHNDC, vice chair of Community Board 8 (Prospect Heights, Crown Heights, and Weeksville), and a Prospect Heights resident since 2000.[3] He is a middle-aged white man. Our wide-ranging conversation highlights how development pressure interacts with the landmarking process from the perspective of someone involved as both an active community member and a professional. It also exemplified who makes up community organizations and how landmarking can function as a source of community organization.

Witherwax lives in a historic brownstone in the Prospect Heights landmark district, but when he originally moved to the neighborhood, he lived in a large apartment building on Eastern Parkway, at the edge of Prospect Heights. In our conversation, he returned repeatedly to his efforts to create a new landmark district for that strip of multifamily buildings, revealing the contrast between the landmarking process and its success or frustration in two physically different parts of the larger neighborhood.

Witherwax began by arguing that "landmarking, among its other salutary values in New York City, is a bulwark against wrong—you know—noncontextual development, out of scale development." Later he insisted that landmarking does not contribute directly to displacement. Indeed, he went so far as to declare, "I think, if anything, it has the opposite effect because it disincentivizes the type of rapacious development that is nakedly about displacement."

Witherwax understands landmarking as a tool for maintaining the integrity of the neighborhood built environment but also for maintaining communities, or at least populations in place. Witherwax conceded that land use zoning regulation[4] can accomplish this too, at least the built environment piece, but said that compared to historic preservation,

> zoning is such a blunt instrument. . . . Where are the mixed use zoning code provisions? Point them [out] to me, because I can't find them. Where are the commercial/manufacturing/ residential overlays? I don't see them anywhere. It's too blunt and city planning is the greater villain in that narrative than LPC ever could be.[5]

The most interesting emphasis in our conversation was Witherwax's sense of the importance of the public process to landmarking, which exposes development decisions to public consideration. He expanded on this, pointing to how this process can restrain speculative development and increase community power:

> A landmark regime [creates] a way to say to the private property owner, "Whoa, stop. We've got a public process and we're not saying, 'no, you can't do this,' we're just going to say 'put your cards on the table.' If the rationale [for the proposed changes] is aesthetic [that's fine, but if] your end game is really that you just want to monetize this property . . . and kick everybody out and throw the old ladies out of the old ladies' home and move in the hedge fund millionaires, then maybe we're going to have something negative to say about that." . . . So that's why I think landmarking is a net positive.

Buying into a historic neighborhood is confirmation of the importance of that neighborhood's integrity and implies a commitment to maintain it.

Witherwax admitted that there can be a downside to this process: "Now it bothers me when people come in and try to redesign other people's windows . . . you gotta watch out, it gives people a little too much interest in other people's business, maybe." That said, he does not believe that the standard complaint—that historic preservation regulations increase the cost of maintaining buildings—goes much beyond the level of inconvenience. He pointed out that landmarking has no impact on many aspects of maintenance. In regard to the large, multifamily buildings at the edge of Prospect Heights, a new frontier for landmarking in Brooklyn, Witherwax argued that there are economies of scale when purchasing materials and the costs are divided among more households. "It's a perception," he said, about increased costs, "that may not be backed up by reality."

Finally, Witherwax addressed the question of who participates in this community process, who joins community organizations like PHNDC and attends meetings of the community board, and how they overlap. Although he rejected the idea that it is only "cranks," he emphasized that the group is "self-selecting":

> It's not the cranks. . . . It's not the rose colored glasses people. . . . It's not even the nostalgists. There's a certain passion for this, which is really hard to understand, because it tends to be repetitive and monotonous. . . . So you have to have that . . . almost masochistic quality to want to put up with that too. You know, by and large it's just a bunch of people who have a good head on their shoulders and who like to work together, and the people who don't play well in the sandbox don't tend to stick around.

Those who select in have developed an amateur interest in historic architectural detail that is entangled with their commitment to and, most commonly, ownership stake in the neighborhood. But they also have to be willing to review the same kinds of applications again and again with consistent attention to detail and a willingness to work toward consensus with their neighbors. Witherwax also explained that formal community board appointments are opaque and a kind of confirmation of the self-selection process because "people who submit their applications seem to kind of get appointed."

Demographically, Witherwax characterized those "who show up and put in the effort" as longtime neighborhood residents of retirement age, often car owners, predominantly women, and, in central Brooklyn, predominantly African American. He noted that, as is true of himself, there are increasing numbers of "new people"—meaning predominantly white—who have been in the neighborhood for twenty years or more and are starting to get involved and that this is changing the complexion of these groups.

My conversation with Ethel Tyus, chair of the Community Board 8 Land Use Committee and founding member of the CHNA, highlighted similar themes.[6] This was not surprising because Witherwax had recommended I speak with her as a longer-time advocate for their larger part of Brooklyn. Tyus reflects the involved neighborhood resident that Witherwax suggests dominates local organizations: somewhat older, African American, and a longtime central Brooklyn resident. She went further than Witherwax in clarifying the specific sources and mechanisms of development pressure and their effects on historic neighborhoods.

Like Witherwax, Tyus immediately connected her work to preserve Crown Heights to the larger development forces in Brooklyn. She sees gentrification in Brooklyn proceeding from skyrocketing rents in Manhattan, a kind of spillover. In the face of this, many longtime homeowners are tempted to sell. Tyus answered the question, "Why do they sell?"

> They don't have the reservoir of maintenance dollars to maintain the property. They're old and tired, tired of the painting and the sweeping the leaves, and all the other entropic changes that happen to older houses that have to be attended to. Every year you have got to do something to keep that house in one piece. So . . . what we see is these older folks, whose kids have moved away, not having the intestinal fortitude to continue to do the property maintenance on the older buildings. And they don't have the legal advice to do a trust or to figure out another way to maintain the property to continue to live there and still get the building taken care of. So they'll sell and they'll go into a nursing home.

In other words, the nature of central Brooklyn's preservation problem stems from the "entropic changes" and the disjunction between the dwindling resources of many longtime Black homeowners, many of whose children have moved away, and the current value of these constantly deteriorating properties.

Tyus explained that New York State historic tax credits particularly benefit neighborhoods that are identified by the U.S. Census as "distressed," a factor that has been important in funding the maintenance of historic houses in central Brooklyn. She is concerned, though, that the 2020 census will show sufficient demographic and economic change in central Brooklyn that the area will no longer qualify as distressed, eliminating that source of support, a perverse consequence of neighborhood change. Indeed, the demographic data I provided in chapter 3 indicate a trajectory of population shift that reinforces Tyus's concern—a decline in Black residents and an increase in educational attainment.

In sum, community preservationists working in neighborhoods where landmarking is well established clarify landmarking's role in resisting neighborhood change in the face of intense development pressure. In particular, landmarking establishes a process through which development decisions are exposed to public consideration, and it can bring together community organizations that address issues beyond the preservation of structures, extending to maintaining populations in place.

COMMUNITY BOARD 3 AD HOC LANDMARKS COMMITTEE

The struggle over development decisions in historic neighborhoods in central Brooklyn plays out at the neighborhood level before just the kind of self-selecting groups of passionate and committed locals that Witherwax described. In Bedford-Stuyvesant, Community Board 3 (CB3) has appointed an ad hoc landmarks committee to supervise the landmarking process. The volunteers on the committee have the authority to review applications and make recommendations to the larger board, which will ultimately vote on those recommendations and forward them to LPC. In 2016, the ad hoc committee included Morgan Muncey, a local realtor and resident, who brought me to the May 9, 2019, meeting of the committee.[7]

The Landmarks Committee gathered in the community board's offices in Restoration Plaza on Fulton Street, a big commercial strip in Bed-Stuy. Restoration Plaza was "rehabilitated in 1972 from its former life as the Sheffield Farms Milk Bottling Plant" by the Bedford-Stuyvesant Restoration Corporation, "the nation's first Community Development organization."[8] It combines a historic, brick industrial building with modern glass and steel elements closer to the street. The community board's office was low ceilinged, fluorescent-lit, and cluttered with information in multiple printed forms to be distributed to constituents. Approximately fifteen men and women, evenly Black and white, squeezed around a large table in mismatched chairs to listen to presentations from local homeowners and their representatives. The meeting was led by two CB3 members, and the attendees were actively involved neighborhood homeowners interested in historic preservation. My arrival with Muncey was apparently enough to certify my presence.

A range of petitions was considered at the May meeting. Among the most revealing of the committee's attitude was a local homeowner's testimony about the activities of Brookland, a developer active in the area.[9] Brookland was building on the site of some historic stables.[10] The homeowner complained that she had to stop workers from tearing up the cobblestone street and then stop them again when they came back to pour concrete over the cobblestones. She explained to the committee that her block had come out strongly in opposition to Brookland's project and would call out any violation, but she expressed the concern that developers had the money to simply pay fines and move on. The committee listened to this report with disquiet, clearly on the same side.

Next the committee reviewed the petition of a developer, Dixon, who I am told owns fifty-six properties in the neighborhood, mostly brownstone row houses that rent for $7,000 to $10,000 per month.[11] Dixon is owned by an Australian financial services firm, a striking example of the role of international capital in the process of gentrification, one to which many of gentrification's critics ascribe great importance.[12] Their petition involved alterations to a historic brownstone in the process of conversion to a luxury, single-family, rental property. One neighbor, in attendance to testify against the proposed changes, argued that "these are family homes, they are not for Jacuzzis."[13] The committee considered the petition with skepticism, but the June interaction is more revealing of the committee's dynamic.

In June 2016, I returned for the monthly meeting.[14] My prior attendance was facilitated by my arrival with Muncey, but there was some skepticism this time about the appropriateness of my presence, despite the fact this was a public meeting posted on the community board's calendar. Why would a neighborhood outsider be interested in the activities of a committee that normally only attracted homeowners making changes, developers, and their architects? After some discussion, a compromise was reached, and I was allowed to stay for the public part of the meeting. But I was asked to leave after the first hour when the committee went into "executive session," a part of the meeting I had observed in May.

The public portion of the June CB3 landmarks committee meeting best reveals the grassroots, local, idiosyncratic, and personality-driven quality of preservation regulation. The group of committed amateur preservationists is racially diverse, but the majority on the committee are Black and female. Much of the conversation about proposed changes turned on committee members' individual experiences with their own houses, although they also argued from an apparently deep knowledge of the neighborhood's architectural history, repeatedly citing the need for a historically coherent district. Their comments, in the aggregate, gave a clear impression that they were trying to slow local development using landmarking regulations.

Among the topics for the night were variance requests in relation to inexpensive, sometimes poorly accomplished repairs that predated the landmark district and are "grandfathered in." Under the law, homeowners are not required to replace them despite the fact that they violate historic integrity. If they do replace them, however, the replacements are required to meet the historic standards. Arguments emerged about whether the way this is currently playing out makes sense. In many cases before the board, homeowners are innocently attempting to improve the look and performance of their houses by replacing these cheap materials and unaesthetic details—metal doors, vinyl windows—without first getting permission. But homeowners are running into the LPC's historic orthodoxy and requirements of specific designs and expensive custom work.

The committee was quite sympathetic to these supplicants coming to them for help dealing with LPC and were critical of LPC, alleging inexperience in balancing preservation with the economic realities facing many homeowners in Bed-Stuy. A middle-aged, white, male resident of Macon Street had replaced his "worn out" modern door without LPC permission.

He explained there was "so much going on" on his street, a reference to extensive redevelopment in the rapidly gentrifying neighborhood, that he did not think anyone would notice, but he has received a warning letter from LPC. The new door is solid wood (thus quite expensive) and stained "golden oak." LPC requires it to be a darker shade and for him to remove the spokes in the fanlight above so it is a single, undivided pane. Clearly irritated, the homeowner ·arrived with plans to make these changes and was consulting with the committee to confirm that they were adequate. The committee seemed positively disposed to the homeowner, recommended he consult the 1940 tax photo of the property, and ultimately agreed that his planned changes should satisfy the landmark district's standards.

The June meeting also involved the petition of a multiunit building owner, also on Macon Street. He came to the committee for help "legalizing" his new wood windows. The owner reported having spent $12,000 on windows and $4,000 for their installation before being told by LPC that the rectangular windows, which replaced rectangular vinyl windows put in by a previous owner, should, in fact, be arched at the top to fit the brick arch above the window. He explained that arched windows would have added an additional $12,000 to his costs.

It came out over the course of a respectful back and forth with the committee that the building in question consists of single-room occupancy rental units (known as SROs).[15] The petitioner buys and renovates SROs in Bed-Stuy, but keeps the current tenants in place while improving the building, sometimes even training the residents in building trades. One of the committee chairs admiringly called this "real low-income housing."

Eventually a member of the committee offered that brick arches are common above windows because late-nineteenth-century builders did not use stone lintels to support the weight of the wall above, but that the original windows would, by his observation, likely have been rectangular. The committee is clearly favorably disposed toward the building owner because of the progressivism of his broader project and promises a letter, in a tone of some outrage, recommending legalization after the fact to LPC. The committee's responses to both of these petitioners reflect balancing historical integrity in design with the practical realities and financial constraints of building ownership.

The committee's attitude to the real estate developers and their representatives who appeared before them was distinctly less friendly. Dixon was on the agenda again. What was most notable about Dixon's presentation was the tone of condescension, control, and only grudging cooperation. The project manager presented the proposed changes to a brownstone on Decatur Street as a fait accompli and used phrases such as "what additions and small changes we *are* making to the property," "we would be willing to consider," and "we are trying to listen to your comments and will try to accommodate [you]." The project manager was neither deferential nor sympathetic to the committee's concerns. For their part, the committee was skeptical of the necessity of adding an elevator and roof deck to the building but framed their criticisms in terms of their assumption that the property was a speculative luxury rental, not being designed for a particular household. A similar attitude toward developers was evident at the May meeting.

The activities of the ad hoc landmarks committee of CB3 in Bed-Stuy reflect the local activism of historically minded residents working to accommodate everyday life within a landmark district and to resist speculative development that speeds an already rapid process of gentrification. Outside forces, embodied by developers, appear to be responsible for this process. The locals experience this as being imposed upon them, which creates a tension I did not observe elsewhere. Among the neighborhoods I explored for my research, Bed-Stuy was the only one in which I was ever threatened, the only one in which my conspicuous middle-class Whiteness seemed to present a challenge or a risk.

CROWN HEIGHTS SOUTH

The development pressure in Crown Heights South is similar to that in Bed-Stuy, but the neighborhood does not have a history of landmarking, from which both Bed-Stuy and Crown Heights North benefit, nor the degree of community cohesion that could underpin a new landmark districting process. Evelyn Tully Costa, founder and president of the Crown Heights South Association described gentrification in the neighborhood as "on steroids" or like "a feeding frenzy."[16] The local, personality-driven process of the practice of historic preservation remains the same in Crown Heights South but reveals some of the weaknesses of this situation.

Tully Costa, president of the CHSA, explained that she is energetically seeking landmark designation for the core of the neighborhood. She has mastered the architectural history of the neighborhood and has begun to identify the contributing buildings to a potential landmark district, but she emphasizes that she repeatedly confronts problems of organization. Her professional experience makes her comfortable in front of a crowd and happy to discuss the details of the landmarking project, but she struggles to find others with whom to share the burden.

Like Ethel Tyus, Tully Costa laments seeing longtime residents, overwhelmingly Black, "cashing out and moving South." Although emphasizing that she could not begrudge them the opportunity, she bemoaned the disappearance of committed community members. She also complained that sixty to seventy people show up for community meetings but the same ten to fifteen are left to do the work. In a later conversation, she described her frustration trying to get others involved in the work of the CHSA:[17]

> I said, "You know what? Don't tell me you're too busy, because the developers are not. They're busy destroying our neighborhood. So either you do the landmarking or you shut up about it, because there's a tool in our arsenal that's been employed by dozens of neighborhood groups around the city to stop this."

Like Spellen, with whom she works, Tully Costa[18] says that "nearby catastrophes help spur locals," meaning that radical changes to historic buildings the community has come to take for granted often draw their attention to the threat of development and the potential protective power of preservation regulation.

Tully Costa stressed the necessity of landmarking in the face of constant and increasing development pressure in Crown Heights South: "The city hasn't done anything except encourage luxury housing. And no, not all boats—what is it? 'All boats rise with the tide?' Does not work. That's trickledown bullshit." Moreover, she uses this as a rallying cry with which to engage others, "either you do the landmarking or you shut up about it." It is not just homeowners, whose properties are potentially affected by the regulations, that should care. Tully Costa believes it is "people in rent stabilized buildings who should want landmarking even more. There's this huge pressure to get them out and, you know, tear down those ratty old buildings and put up something shiny, new, and cheap, which none of them will be able to afford to live in."

Tully Costa argued that the essence of a "stable neighbor-hood" is that speculative sales and development have been discouraged. Landmarking, she realizes, can only go so far to stabilize Crown Heights (my Prospect Heights interviewees made a similar point). As property prices increase, so do property taxes, which sometimes push the costs of continuing to own out of reach of low- and middle- income homeowners. The pressure associated with increasing costs is compounded by what Tully Costa describes as harassment at the hands of "predatory real estate scammers," who call, leaflet, and visit homes in the hopes of persuading homeowners to sell, so they can, in turn, flip or redevelop the property. Landmarking, unfortunately from Tully Costa's perspective, does not affect the ability to buy and sell. It does, however, constrain redevelopment and can make available new resources to help low- and middle- income homeowners maintain their properties.

Landmarking does prevent one specific hazard for renters. Tully Costa explained a phenomenon associated with changing prices and development pressure that she calls "demolition evic-tion." A landlord can evict even rent-stabilized tenants if they have an alternative plan for the building site, demonstrate fund-ing for the new plan, and have agreed to pay relocation expenses for tenants. But then, Tully Costa explained, "there's no penalty for not doing the building." There are no consequences for fail-ing to carry out the plans that were the rationale for the evic-tions. The landlord can find new tenants who pay higher rents. This would only be worth the trouble in a neighborhood where rents were increasing rapidly. Landmarking would eliminate this strategy because demolishing contributing buildings in land-mark districts is prohibited.

Tully Costa offered all of these reasons to explain why she has been seeking landmark designation for the core of Crown

Heights South. She firmly believes landmarking is a powerful tool, claiming that it preserves "not just the buildings, but the people too." Slowing development reduces financial pressure on the neighborhood and discourages the kind of speculative development most closely associated with displacement.

Tully Costa has connected to and is drawing upon the experience of the Crown Heights North Association to guide her efforts, and she anticipates a lengthy process. But Tully Costa is acutely aware that part of the difference in the landmarking processes in Crown Heights North (successful, multiple phases) and South (as yet not designated) is attributable to the built environment of the respective neighborhoods. Crown Heights North "was developed, starting in the eighteen forties, as practically a playground for the rich. . . . So they have a much more elegant upscale building stock." She connects both the neighborhood's gentrification and organization to this elegant stock. Most of Crown Heights South, in contrast, was developed between 1900 and 1930, for middle and upper-middle class professionals, "a car neighborhood for people who could afford a car." Its built environment is less aesthetically distinct and is less likely to facilitate the kind of casual sociability that builds community.

Advocating for a landmark district in Crown Heights South requires community organizing, according to Tully Costa.

> First, we have to go around and get the support and explain this process to people. And then, LPC, when they're starting to do this project, they want to show up to meetings and hear neighbors say, "yes." If we've done our job of educating people ahead of all this, landmarks will get a positive response. So our job is to educate our neighbors: "If you don't do this, that's what you get [referring to new development and displacement]. And if you do this, you get a stable neighborhood."

She seems optimistic on this front, remarking that landmarking's importance is increasingly recognized. A key reason is the knowledge that other neighborhoods that "*could* do it, *have done* it."

Tully Costa was careful to delineate the various technical steps, such as drawing district boundaries, doing a building survey, and producing a report. These are substantially community processes as well because the labor of a building survey needs to be shared. Moreover, district boundaries must include both historically appropriate buildings and cooperative property owners. The Crown Heights South landmarking effort contends with a number of issues particular to it.

Foremost, the broader neighborhood includes a significant community of Lubavitcher Jews or Chabad Hasidim, who often build significant additions to their houses to accommodate large families and, accordingly, resist landmarking restrictions. Any district boundary for Crown Heights South must be drawn in a way that does not include the homes of the neighborhood's substantial Lubavitcher population. This is essential for the process of organizing community support. Toward this end, Tully Costa has drawn the boundaries of the initial proposed landmark district to avoid the Lubavitchers' part of the neighborhood.[19] Second, the Bedford Union Armory, a large historic structure that could potentially anchor a landmark district, is caught up in a debate about its future use. Tully Costa and landmarking advocates are arguing for a community center, but the city's preferred plans include more changes to the structure and extensive affordable housing, which Tully Costa calls (like Bankoff) a "Trojan horse."[20]

Finally, my interviews with Tully Costa, like my interview with Tyus, point to the critical role of particular individuals in community organizations and how they constitute organizational capacity, at least in the early stages. Community organizations are founded on the excitement and energy of individuals, and they frequently develop according to the personal and professional capacities of those people. The personal impulse of organization can prove to be a limitation as well because those organizations frequently rely entirely on those same people and the idiosyncrasies of their lives. In this regard, biography proves critical to understanding both progress and stagnation in the landmarking process.

The trajectory of landmarking in Crown Heights South is illustrative. By the second time I spoke with Tully Costa, she had significantly reduced her role in CHSA because of health issues, which compromised the organization's progress. Tully Costa lamented that

> the logjam we're hitting is, unfortunately, my health. I basically said to my board about a month or two ago . . . I need to step back a little and you guys need to fill in some blanks and do more of the work. So we're in the process now of hopefully getting some people trained up to do the [landmark district] presentations and just get out there and meet community members. They're all a little shy. . . . Because I happen to come from a preservation background, I'm not shy about speaking to people. So I've been doing it, but I haven't really been effective because I'm, like, sick half the time.

Her comments point to a key weakness of a personality-driven process: different members, even when equally committed, may have different levels of skill. Tully Costa's professional formation, as well as her extroverted personality, have meant that she is effective as the face of the organization, facilitating outreach and spreading the message—she is almost individually responsible for much of the organization's impact to date. At the same time, her chronic illness limits her ability to fulfill this role, and no one in the organization is capable of or willing to assume her responsibilities.

Moreover, although Tully Costa has dedicated her time to the organization, some of the people with whom she has attempted to share the workload are not as available (or possibly as dedicated): "We're supposed to be doing . . . a building survey [to prepare for the landmarking application]. But the woman that said she could do it got a full-time job, so I haven't heard from her in three months." In addition to personality and professional formation, community organizing requires time, which in turn requires resources.

The Bedford Union Armory

Redevelopment of the Bedford Union Armory offers another illustration of the functions and processes of historic preservation in Central Brooklyn, and it vividly illuminates the aggressive development (or redevelopment) pressures faced by communities there. My research into the recent history of the redevelopment of the Bedford Union Armory was archival in nature.[21] I point out important aspects of the redevelopment process, highlighting the roles of local politicians and their relationship to community groups and their susceptibility to pressure. Most important, the Bedford Union Armory story is one of *failure*. Landmark preservation fails to win the day, forced into the background by the tension between for-profit development and the creation of affordable housing that dominates the New York City landscape.

The Bedford Union Armory in Crown Heights South was built in 1903. The New York State Department of Environmental

Conservation describes the site as "undeveloped before 1903, was used as an armory from about 1904 until sometime before 2013, when control of the property was relinquished to the city." "The property was also occasionally used for film productions between 1991 and 2012."[22] The Bedford Union Armory's closure is significant because the site is now city-owned, in the middle of a rapidly redeveloping area, is large for central Brooklyn, and includes a structure that could easily be repurposed as a recreation center, but also has space for other facilities.

In late 2013, the New York City Economic Development Corporation (NYCEDC), announced a request for proposals to "reactivate" the armory. NYCEDC is a nonprofit corporation with a board appointed by the mayor and borough presidents that promotes business in New York City under contract with the city government. Initially, it was not clear what reactivating the armory would mean for the surrounding neighborhoods, but in December 2015, NYCEDC announced, in cooperation with Brooklyn Borough President Eric Adams and City Council Member Laurie Cumbo, that the armory would be sold as a "500,000 Square Foot Mixed-Use Development."[23] Initial reaction to the plan by local residents was positive. Evelyn Tully Costa told me, "This is the place that our community needs to come together. Those kids should have the same things that I had growing up in Fairfield, Connecticut."[24] Tully Costa anticipated, and suggested this was a widespread expectation, that the project would include a recreation center to serve the neighborhood, but she also hoped the project could proceed without damaging the historic details of the building itself.

The devil has proved to be in other details. Over the nearly eleven-month period following the announcement, resistance gathered in the neighborhood to the plans that emerged. Unfortunately, the details of the action on the ground and the discussions that must have taken place went uncovered by local media. By October 2016, NYCEDC's intentions for the proposed redevelopment were becoming clear. The project was described in *The Guardian* in the following terms:[25]

> Currently, the developer selected by the EDC, BFC Partners, plans to redevelop the site with a 13-story building with 300 rental apartments and 24 condominiums, along with a state-of-the-art recreational center that will be open to the community in some capacity. Of the 300 apartments, 18 will be reserved for households earning no more than 40 percent of average median income (AMI), which is defined by the city as just over $36,000 for a family of four; another 49 will be set aside for households making no more than 50 percent of AMI ($45,000 for a family of four). The developer will reserve 99 units for households making no more than 110 percent of AMI (about $100,000 for a family of four), and the remaining 164 units will go at market rates to those with the minimum income to qualify.

The neighborhood's expectation that a city-owned property would be redeveloped to benefit the community was undermined by the large number of market rate rental units and what were described elsewhere as luxury condominiums incorporated in the plan. The prominent inclusion of these units intensified already-present fears of gentrification.

This time, presumably in response to community dissatisfaction, local elected officials weighed in against the project. As reported in *The Guardian*,

> US congresswoman Yvette Clarke, state senator Jesse Hamilton, state assemblyman Walter Mosley and state assemblywoman Diana Richardson released a letter they had written to the

president and CEO of the New York City economic development corporation (EDC) asking that "the community's voice is both heard and acted upon" as the project progresses.

Among other things, U.S. Congresswoman Clarke emphasized, "At a time when gentrification threatens many longtime residents with displacement, we need a comprehensive approach that significantly and substantially addresses all of the community's needs." What this framing—affordability vs. profit, community vs. development—misses is the historic nature of the building. This fits with Bankoff's argument that historic preservation and affordability so often wind up falsely opposed in New York City (see chapter 3).

This begins a lengthy period of reconsideration of the project in which the resistance of both local politicians and local residents becomes more visible. Within weeks, the same group of four elected officials (all of them representing the neighborhood, but none of them responsible for decisions about the armory's future) took a public stance that would define the terms of the debate about the redevelopment of the armory going forward: that a project redeveloped on city-owned land should include 100 percent affordable housing. They followed this with a Freedom of Information Act request for the project's financials in an effort to expose the revenue and expense calculations the developer claimed required the presence of substantial market rate housing to support the recreation center.

In a measure of significant political division, Smith writes about this request:[26]

Notably absent from the letter are the two local officials who have approval power over the project, Councilmember Laurie Cumbo and Brooklyn Borough President Eric Adams, who will review the plans as part of the Uniform Land Use Review Procedure, set to begin this spring.

Tully Costa told me she thought Cumbo was "under a lot of pressure to reconsider the deal."[27]

By March of 2017, community opposition was growing in magnitude and visibility. In late February Tully Costa told me that "the good news is there's huge community opposition to this thing." In the month that followed, two local media sources, *Gothamist* and *Curbed*, reported vocal community opposition in community meetings, clarifying that the primary concern remains housing affordability: "Throughout the course of the meeting, attendees challenged the developer's narrative of affordability, pointing out that only the 18 units targeted at the lowest income bracket would be affordable for the average family in Crown Heights."[28]

In late March, arguments about affordability came to incorporate concerns about a racial transition. *Curbed* publicized a new report by New York Communities for Change, a housing affordability advocacy group, suggesting that "Bedford-Union Armory redevelopment won't benefit residents of color." "Rather, the Bedford Courts development will accelerate the whitening of Crown Heights, with fewer affordable apartments available for residents of color who earn lower incomes, and more apartments geared toward whiter, wealthier newcomers to the neighborhood." It also notes support for the project from one of the nonprofit organizations that will benefit from the affordable office space the armory will provide, West Indian American Day Carnival Association.[29]

A month later, the armory developers announced that they would use union labor and provide training programs for local residents,[30] presumably hoping to appease the community. City

Council Member Laurie Cumbo announced that this was not enough and finally took a formal stand on the project, coming out against it in May 2017. Her decision built on statements over several months indicating that "Cumbo . . . wasn't satisfied by the amount of affordable housing being offered in the project." According to *Politico*, those statements and her ultimate position were a response to community opposition and the fear of a primary challenge, using the armory development project as a key issue:

> Cumbo has been the target of community protests over the plan, including demonstrations outside her district office. Sources said the external pressure had contributed to her earlier reluctance to publicly embrace the plan, even as she expressed a desire for some type of development at the site. . . . Crown Heights residents and others opposed to the project are planning to protest Cumbo at her State of the District Thursday, citing Cumbo's lack of clarity over a community plan which was presented to her as part of an effort to include more affordable housing than what is currently proposed in the project. Cumbo, a first-term Council member, is not only facing community opposition but also a primary challenger running for her seat. Former City Council staffer Ede Fox is challenging Cumbo and is making the armory issue a central part of her campaign.[31]

Curbed reported her new position under the title, "Controversial Bedford-Union Armory Redevelopment Loses Cumbo's Support," shortly before her State of the District speech.

> "I stand here today with my colleagues in government to demand Mayor de Blasio go back to the drawing board and produce a plan that meets the needs of my Brooklyn neighbors," Cumbo said in

a statement. "It's important that we have a developer that helps enhance our community, meets with the trade unions, commits to hiring locally, and builds this project with the highest safety standards available."[32]

This news was followed in relatively quick succession by the unanimous rejection of the armory redevelopment project by the Community Board 9 Land-Use Subcommittee and the entire Community Board 9 (the local, appointed citizen advisory board).[33] The relative lack of affordable housing in the plan for the armory appears to have been critical in both of these votes.

These votes posed significant obstacles to the project because the first step in planning and permitting development requires city council approval. City council members, however, generally accept the guidance of their community boards on local issues, and the council as a whole follows the lead of the member representing the area in which a project is proposed.

The armory project continued to face significant resistance over the summer and into the early fall. A hearing in July 2017, led by Brooklyn Deputy Borough President Diana Reyna as part of the land use review process, was called off after "protestors came out *en masse*."[34] Then in early September, "after hearing from 'thousands of community voices' on the redevelopment of the Bedford-Union Armory in Crown Heights, Brooklyn Borough President Eric Adams" declared that the "Bedford-Union Armory redevelopment should not have condos."[35] Later in September, the developers and representatives from the city agencies supporting the development faced tough questions from the city planning commission. They also confronted opposition testimony from New York State Assembly Representative Diana Richardson, and a representative of New York Communities for Change—the source of the report on the risk of racial transition

or racial preferences built into the plans for affordability—testi-
fied to concerns that the city planning commissioners had not
pushed hard enough on the affordability question.[36]

Up to this point, the conversation about the armory seemed
to suggest that it would not proceed without a major reassess-
ment, that community resistance, channeled through local
appointed and elected officials from multiple advisory and legislative bodies, constituted an immovable obstacle. Reinforcing
this view, another *Politico* article suggested that three of Mayor
de Blasio's attempted neighborhood rezonings were frustrated
by the city council in response to local opposition (Cobble Hill,
Inwood, and Sunnyside).[37]

Readers familiar with New York City development politics
will not be surprised to learn that this was not the end of the
story. Despite community friction and official opposition, the
city planning commission approved the armory proposal in late
October. *Curbed* reported, "Despite protestors disrupting the
meeting, the City Planning Commission approved the embattled conversion of the Bedford-Union Armory at a meeting
on Monday." Based on promises from the developers that they
would continue to work with Council Member Laurie Cumbo
and "other stakeholders to ensure this project serves the Crown
Heights community," the plan passed eleven to one.[38]

Cumbo subsequently negotiated changes to the plan that
eliminated the luxury condominiums and secured additional
low-income housing units. On November 21, 2017, Cumbo
explained the new plan and her decision to support it to the
city council land use committee and planning subcommittee.
Brooklyn Reader covered Cumbo's statements about the revised
plan at length.

"Today, I am proud to announce my support for a dramatically
revised Bedford Union Armory project, which will provide the

greatest level of low-income and affordable housing that the Crown Heights community has seen in decades," said Cumbo. "I fought to remove 48 luxury condominiums, deepened the bands of affordability by securing approximately 250 housing units for low-income and formerly homeless families—quadrupling the affordable housing that was proposed in the original plan, with at least $1.25 million annually in programmatic engagement at the Armory."[39]

The subsequent subcommittee vote was unanimous in its support of the project. A little more than a week later, the city council approved the plan. The *Brooklyn Paper* similarly attributes Cumbo's "change of heart" to these concessions:

> The city and developer also agreed to expand the project's so-called affordable housing component from 166 to 250 units, and reduced the prices of those apartments—which originally ran as high as around $2,300 per month—to between approximately $640 and $1,280 per month. But BFC Partners will still be allowed to build 149 market-rate rentals on the site as part of the revised proposal.[40]

But Cumbo's deal did not satisfy everyone, and enough local opposition to the plan remained that the city council vote was interrupted by protesters shouting "The city is not for sale! Kill the deal!" and "Laurie lies!" as security escorted them out of the chamber. Still, *Gotham Gazette* reflects that "by all accounts, the pressure moved the needle significantly. . . . BFC cut out the condos as the city promised $50 million to subsidize more affordable—and more deeply affordable—rental housing on the site."[41]

Community dissenters, despite their political loss, had one final hope for delaying, if not overturning, the project. The day before the city council approved the new deal, the Legal Aid Society filed suit against the city alleging that the city's environmental review process failed to project the impact of new, market rate housing on local rent-regulated tenants. The fact that it had made such projections for market rate tenants likely to be affected, the suit argued, was insufficient.[42] Jennifer Levy, supervising attorney of the Legal Aid Society, explained that "they don't measure indirect displacement in the way that they should. . . . We know from looking all around us that large-scale projects that introduce higher income people into the community does, in fact, have a displacement effect on rent-regulated units." She also questioned the legitimacy of the armory project's proposed community advisory board (another of the developers' concessions to Cumbo), maintaining it would be a "closed oversight mechanism," appointed by the developers.[43]

The suit would come up short when it was finally decided in July 2018. In the decision, "state Supreme Court Justice Carmen Victoria St. George ruled that the city's review guidelines provide an adequate perspective on the environmental impact of developments—even when community members disagree with the outcome." The article quoted the judge's decision:

> "The court is sympathetic to petitioners, who aim to protect those who are not members of community boards, are not elected officials, and often do not express their positions at public hearings." St. George wrote. "The goal of the city, and of the projects at hand, is to balance the interests of communities . . . this court's role, in turn, is not to question the way in which the city, entrusted with these projects, draws the balance."[44]

Months before the case was settled, in mid-March 2018, BFC filed a permit application for a fifteen-story building on the site.[45] In the rendering, the building is shown where the garage and parking were previously. As proposed, it is intended to include "355 units, 190 of which will be affordable and 165 market rate." According to a spokesperson for the developer, it will also have "below ground parking for 201 cars and 178 bicycles." The application also included a second eight-story building for low-income housing.[46]

Brooklyn Paper reported that the eight-story "building's 60 apartments will be among the complex's total 250 below-market-rate rentals, which will be offered to families and individuals making 30 to 60 percent of the area's medium income, and include 25 units reserved for formerly homeless people."[47] The project will be called "Bedford Courts" and "the plans list Marvel Architects as the applicant of record, and the city's Economic Development Corporation as the owner."[48]

The Armory's "head house" (which previously contained sleeping quarters, showers, artillery ranges, stables, and kitchen and laundry areas) was maintained in roughly its original state (new purpose as yet unclear), and the drill hall had become the recreation center. The architectural details of both apartment buildings were revised going forward, primarily in terms of superficial detail, although also in the massing of the smaller building.

This application, however, was rejected without prejudice in May 2018, shortly before the court's decision.[49] The fifteen-story building has yet to be resubmitted for permitting approval, although none of the articles covering steps toward the armory's development mention any further resistance beyond the Legal Aid suit that was decided in July of 2018.

In September 2018, *Curbed* covered an announcement that the State of New York would contribute $15 million to the armory's planned community center and name it in honor of

Carey Gabay, one of Governor Cuomo's aides "who was killed by a stray bullet during the J'ouvert celebrations in 2015." In addition to sports facilities, "the community center will also be home to seven community-based organizations, with a social services-based organization anchoring this group. Finally, the community center will also house the Carey Gabay Foundation, which is run by his wife, Trenelle Gabay."[50] Most recently, on April 15, 2019, City Council Majority Leader Laurie Cumbo announced, in cooperation with the developers, the establishment of the Bedford Union Armory advisory committee.

> The committee will serve as a liaison between the community and EDC/BFC, guiding the Armory's management to develop programs that will best serve the welfare of the neighborhood's youth and families. The committee will be comprised of 15 members, including the Chair, with local elected officials, community groups and BFC appointing eight of the members, while the remaining 7 will come from a pool of local stakeholders and be open to the public.[51]

The actual composition of the committee and its impact on the project remain to be seen.

Redevelopment of the Bedford Union Armory is one more story about the various ways local communities attempt to use the preservation of historic resources to stem the tide of aggressive development and gentrification. This time, however, we see the significant role played by community organizations and elected politicians as well as the complex structures of decision making within city government. In the context of intense development pressure in central Brooklyn, it is another story about the importance of individual players in the political process, the development process, and where they intersect. Here,

Laurie Cumbo managed to position herself so that requests to shape the project, both from above (the developer and city) and below (Crown Heights community groups and affordable housing advocates), had to go through her—she mediated them, connected them, moderated their conflicts and overlaps, and, ultimately, determined the outcome almost unilaterally. That outcome, although not satisfactory to some local residents, does add to the supply of low- and middle-income housing in Crown Heights, potentially preserving the local community in the face of increasing property prices. It will also provide much needed recreational amenities, which can either serve a long under-served community or draw new higher-income people into the neighborhood, or both.

The levers that proved effective in shifting the position of Cumbo and other elected politicians were related to affordable housing finance. Community demands for affordable housing were met with resistance from both the developer and the city and were articulated through market logic. When the community itself asks for affordable housing, it is difficult for politicians to refuse, but the necessity to pay for such services is real. At the same time, the original inclusion of luxury condos was tone-deaf, given pressing issues of affordability throughout the city that seem particularly salient in neighborhoods in transition like Crown Heights South. Thus the state's willingness to contribute to the cost of redevelopment made the compromise possible but likely to please no one. It made inclusion of the demanded affordable housing possible, kicking the question of the precise definition of affordability down the road, and it also addressed the developer's concerns about covering costs.

Obscured in all of this back and forth, but central to Evelyn Tully Costa's concerns, is that the armory is a historic land-mark, informally, central to the history of the neighborhood and integral to its historic fabric. As a large, city-owned property, affordable housing advocates see the armory as a rare opportunity to undertake a project with tremendous community benefits without having to first secure the land. Truly affordable housing would avoid the displacement effects that development seems to inflict upon the neighborhood, but redevelopment risks eliminating the armory's historic integrity. The best outcome, from Tully Costa's perspective, would be to accomplish both goals—serving community needs and preserving the structure in its historic state. So far preservation has been ignored in the process, which has been framed in the most conventional terms for New York City as a conflict between affordability and market rate development. If the redevelopment of the armory is undertaken with no sensitivity to its historic design, that might undermine future claims for a landmark district in the neighborhood.

CONCLUSION

In central Brooklyn, landmarking is a strategy to preserve community in the face of intense development pressure. It has had mixed results but remains one of the few tools available to concerned local residents struggling to stay put in a bullish real estate market. As both Witherwax and Tyus attest, landmarking efforts often serve as the basis of broader community outreach, enabling groups to support longtime residents and businesses in ways they might not otherwise. But, as Tully Costa reports, the struggle to get over the organizational hump with a landmarking effort, like the one in Crown Heights South in which she has been involved, is often compounded by the reputation of historic preservation as elitist and aesthetic, whatever the precise truth of the matter. This reputation puts preservation into conflict with discourses on housing affordability. Claims about increased maintenance costs are the obvious example, but this conflict also emerged in connection with the armory. Locals asserted that the primary purpose to which a historic resource should be put is affordable housing and recreation, pushing preservation concerns into the background.

The stories of these central Brooklyn neighborhoods demonstrate how broader economic struggles over the tension between housing development to address shortages and housing affordability to prevent displacement play out at the local level of city government. They illustrate, moreover, the degree to which these local processes are shaped by the individuals involved—individuals who play complex roles in organizing, preservation, and development processes. Their influence on the process, in turn, is dependent on the kinds of professional and personal capital they can bring to bear. Both Witherwax and Tyus are trained as attorneys. This proved central to their roles in PHNDC and CHNA, respectively. Tully Costa's design and preservation training facilitates her ability to present to large groups, but her role as a White in-mover compromised aspects of her organizing ability, whereas Tyus's position as a longtime Brooklynite Black woman enhanced hers. Cumbo's election is too complex to pursue here, but she convinced her constituency that her personal characteristics put her in the right position to represent them. The role of individual personalities and skills is similarly evident in my observation of the CB3 landmarks committee and my reconstruction of the armory redevelopment timeline.

It would be a mistake, however, to overlook how these individuals and their particular accumulations of social capital function within organizational structures. Strong organizations can elevate the organizational above the individual. This is most evident in Cumbo's case—as a pivot point between citywide powers and community efforts, anyone in her position would wield a comparable ability to determine outcomes like that of the armory project. But the organizations are also complicatedly connected by individuals who play roles within many of them, their organizational autonomy perhaps undermined by their reliance on the engaged minority. Witherwax, because of his willingness to serve in multiple roles (PHNDC and CB8), jokes that "pretty soon I'm going to be asking myself for permission for things."[52]

In central Brooklyn, I have looked at landmarking as an embodied social process that takes place at the local level. Landmarking is a complex process through which neighborhood residents sometimes succeed and sometimes fail to influence the changes to their built environment. Rather than diminishing the importance of landmarking, this observation reinforces it. Unlike land use zoning, another process capable of shaping the urban built environment, the landmarking process is consistently initiated from below and is therefore likely to produce outcomes more closely reflective of broader community interests and preferences.

6

CONCLUSION

What is the relationship between historic preservation and neighborhood change? "It's complicated"
understates the case, but we have to begin there
because, at some level, that is the most important contribution
of this book. Historic district designation is treated by many
planners and real estate economists and by many laypeople as if
it had a singular and uniform effect, regardless of the history of
the city or neighborhood in question. My data reveal not only
that this is incorrect but also that it is a fundamental misunderstanding of historic designation. Historic designation is a
dynamic and interactive process that *must* vary from place to
place and moment to moment because it is rooted in the built
environment as a social process (figure 6.1).

This conclusion follows from both the diverse quantitative
data I presented on Baltimore and the qualitative accounts of
preservation activists in Brooklyn. In Baltimore, historic districts are demographically different from never-designated parts
of the city, but how they are different is not consistent across
neighborhoods, nor across time periods. They appear to change
over time, and designation seems to do *something*. In some
instances, I observed the relationship as fortification; that is,

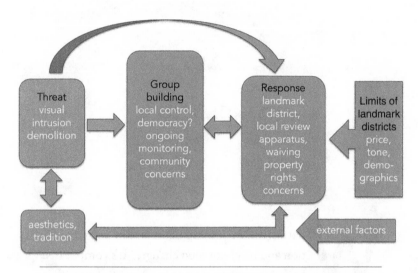

FIGURE 6.1 Conceptual model of landmark districting dynamics

using historic designation to consecrate the relatively higher status of longtime, high-status neighborhoods. This exclusionary practice was exercised in some areas to secure racially restrictive covenants like Roland Park. In Original Northwood, though, something like fortification occurred in conjunction with the neighborhood's transition from majority White to majority Black while improving its educated, upper-middle class profile. In other neighborhoods, such as formerly working-class White Canton, we see something like gentrification following upon historic designation. Finally, in Baltimore, we see a historic tax credit geographically distributed in ways that defy expectation but that may ultimately reflect the institutional capacity in neighborhoods.

The difficulty of doing preservation in a legacy city inflects much of what we understand about Baltimore. All of the efforts to fortify or revitalize are going on in the context of intense vacancy and abandonment reaching back decades. This shrunken and still shrinking city effect is confounded by the contemporary commitment to systematic demolition. However, Project CORE is a program hobbled by legal procedures that shows no signs yet of significantly threatening Baltimore's historic texture. In fact, CORE's primary legacy may prove to be the direction of rehabilitation funds into neighborhoods in ways that reverse some physical decline. Baltimore preservationists are philosophical about CORE's impact, but the program's very design points to the enduring power of the development paradigm, even in a city that has been shrinking for almost seventy years.

This book could not provide a portrayal of what preservation looks like from the perspective of the residents of diverse neighborhoods in Baltimore. With my research substantially complete, I managed to secure a meeting with a neighborhood activist in Easterwood, Baltimore.[1] "Doc" Cheatham gave me a whole morning, walking the streets of the neighborhood, explaining its history and its present, and discussing historic designation and Project CORE, among other things. It quickly became clear that, even for someone with strong connections to the city, day-to-day issues of homelessness, abandonment, physical upkeep, and street crime overwhelmed the policy concerns and funding sources I came to inquire about. Late in this process I also secured a meeting with an officer of the Union Square Association (see chapter 4).[2] The leadership of this organization is now predominantly white and professional, but they still wrestle with issues of abandonment and revitalization. These on-the-ground perspectives—experiences and motivations that drive the actions that manifest as historic district designation or applications for rehabilitation funding through Project CORE—are what we need to know more about to come closer to a complete picture of preservation in Baltimore.

In Brooklyn, I began from a place that must undermine the conventional assumption by being a kind of posterchild for gentrification in recent decades—a city of such intense development pressure that gentrification always seems to come first, always seems to be the dynamic to which community action, regulation, and policy respond. Landmark district designation becomes, in this context, one of the few options communities find to exert some control over the market-driven process of neighborhood change. It also becomes a mechanism for community building because it requires engagement and cooperation among neighbors. Even where this seems consistent, the social processes from which it emerges and its effectiveness vary from neighborhood to neighborhood, differing with phases of gentrification, architectural style and development history, demographics, and the identity and social capital of those who commit themselves to the process.

To understand central Brooklyn better still, we need more information about the results of efforts to mitigate gentrification through landmark district designation. Will it constrain property prices in Bed-Stuy or increase them? Who is moving into central Brooklyn, and is the historic built environment a motivating factor? Finer-grained data on these pushes and pulls—more first person accounts that capture experience and motivation—would help. Charting trajectories is also important; the Bedford-Union Armory is one among many unfinished stories examined here. The impact in central Brooklyn neighborhoods on real estate prices and demographic transitions during the economic downturn in 2020 following the coronavirus crisis also remains to be seen.

We can agree that the relationship between historic preservation and neighborhood change in Baltimore is about maintaining status and facilitating revitalization, whereas in Brooklyn it is a matter of mitigating gentrification and claiming some degree of community control. Baltimore and central Brooklyn are not precisely the ends of a spectrum of urban trajectories, but they do represent radically different urban contexts, kinds of cities, that reveal broader differences in how preservation efforts can manifest and their policy potential. Placing them on some kind of a spectrum enables contrast, and we need to rejoice in this contrast rather than declaring it anomalous. We also need to recognize the idiosyncrasies and interdependencies of these accounts. The relationships between preservation and neighborhood change may be as I describe, but mine is not a complete explanation, nor does it identify an independent mechanism.

The depth of the contrast between Baltimore and Brooklyn could be about the insufficiencies of my method, the incompleteness of my account. But it is more likely that my characterization of top-down processes in one city and bottom-up processes in the other is roughly accurate, despite my preference for telling a more encouraging story about legacy city Baltimore. The governance of a legacy city in a long era of federal urban policy withdrawal is often about trying anything and everything, and in Baltimore's defense, I have not observed any top-down policy that seemed to further disempower its residents.

In the broadest sense, my research points to the radical specificity and contingency of urban dynamics in the United States. The careful examination of historic district designation processes in Baltimore and Brooklyn reinforces this by revealing that local preservation policies may share principles but that designation processes vary according to the history and composition of neighborhoods and cities. Neighborhoods are particular, and the trajectories along which they change (or remain the same) are substantially specific to them. This should not discourage us as urban scholars but reinvigorate our attention to local dynamics, particularly in conversation with any national scale or interurban comparative work. It is another call for the necessity of bridging the micro and macro by digging deeper into the micro.

If we can move beyond the conventional assumption that historic preservation causes gentrification, we can consider all of the diverse things it does do—the purposes it does serve in contemporary U.S. cities beyond those for which it was intended. Preservation may serve indirectly as a mechanism for revitalization in the presence of historic tax credits. It is difficult to characterize their distribution in Baltimore, and I found no connection between tax credit–linked investment and neighborhood change. However, indications are that these credits facilitate investment in (some) historic neighborhoods. I have de-emphasized the importance of the federal rehabilitation tax credit because it rarely applies to owner-occupied residences, but I will remind you that Ryberg-Webster and Kinahan identify it as the second largest source of federal subsidy for most cities, behind only the Community Development Block Grant.[3] Like the CDBG, the federal rehabilitation tax credit reflects the withdrawal of the federal government from an affirmative urban policy and reveals what Hackworth calls "the logic of local autonomy."[4] There is good evidence to connect local preservation policy, historic tax credits, and investment, but the outcome of this investment is less clear.

More important for my purposes and more novel is the observation that historic district designation serves as the basis for important community organizing efforts. Although we cannot see that in my Baltimore data, it is conspicuous in Prospect Heights, Crown Heights North, and Bed-Stuy, each in different ways. Designation as community action is generally important for building neighborhood social capital, as in PHNDC's efforts to shape the Atlantic Yards project, but different and more important in neighborhoods that have been historically marginalized and still face greater challenges associated with that marginalization. CHNA's role is different from PHNDC's because of the demographics and history of the neighborhood and because of the founders of the organization. Brown-Puryear and Young refer to efforts to respond collectively to predatory lending that targeted elders in Crown Heights North,[5] whereas Ethel Tyus talked to me about working with commercial landowners to stabilize neighborhood services for longtime residents. They are working to preserve the benefits of neighborhood revitalization for people who have lived through decades of disinvestment.

The Brooklyn accounts show the limits to the kind of control that organized communities can exercise over their neighborhood through designation, even if they have built intensive connections and pursued a kind of preservation of community. Foremost among these limits is the inability to concretely intervene in the real estate market (which, of course, confirms our sense that the conventional account is missing something). They can instruct their neighbors in the kind of allowable and appropriate alterations to the architectural styles associated with the neighborhood, but they cannot keep their neighbors from selling to wealthy in-movers and moving away. Nor would they want to necessarily, although those who remain bemoan the changes that come with the changing demographics of the neighborhood. Landmark district designation is an imperfect mechanism for communities to use to intervene in the gentrification processes they see going on around them in part because it was not intended for that purpose.

The difficulties of organizing are also essential to acknowledge, prior even to recognizing the limits of designation. In Crown Heights South, the desire to intervene in the development process as their neighbors to the north do is frustrated, as is the ability to shape the process of redevelopment of the Bedford-Union Armory. The difficulty of organizing often comes down to the presence of individuals like Evelyn Tully Costa who has the personal and interpersonal wherewithal to effect community action. When those individuals confront reversals of their own, however, the cost to the organizing process can be profound.

A cautionary note, though, lest the reader perceive me as championing the community organizing potential of the designation process uncritically: Bankoff, of the Historic Districts Council, identified the risk of NIMBY implicit in some designation efforts. Chadotsang, too, in his time at LPC, saw designation undertaken to exclude. As David Harvey and Thomas Sugrue have both identified in writing about very different topics, community organization can often accomplish regressive ends.[6] This again returns us to the necessity of attention to specific examples as opposed to presuming a positive and uniform effect emerging from the community organizing aspect of designation efforts.

Many questions about the relationship between historic preservation and neighborhood change remain unanswered. The most obvious are about what this relationship looks like in other cities and other neighborhoods. Having identified complication, I want to call for further efforts to complicate, and work like this is beginning to emerge.[7] We need both broader and deeper understandings of the variation in preservation policy, the purposes to which preservation regulation is put, the diverse outcomes of designation efforts, popular conceptions of preservation, and the motivations for pursuing it.

Some questions pertaining to the cities that I have explored here also deserve additional attention. What will Project CORE ultimately produce? Will more Baltimore neighborhoods capitalize on the kinds of change that some have accomplished as others continue to shrink? Are there other neighborhoods in Brooklyn (and the rest of New York) that embody interesting stories about preservation as an exercise in community organizing and mitigation?

Throughout this research, I struggled with the intellectual problem of my "most different" comparison. My next step will be to find the middle of that spectrum, and I propose a city roughly halfway between New York and Baltimore in many ways. Philadelphia has an extensive historic built environment, similar to both Baltimore and Brooklyn in important respects. Philadelphia experienced radical shrinkage similar to that of Baltimore, losing more than a quarter of its population between 1950 and 2005. This has left large swaths of the city, mostly dense blocks of brick row houses near industrial sites in North Philadelphia, partly empty and plagued by abandonment similar to parts of Baltimore. But the population trend in Philadelphia has turned around, and the city has been growing for more than a decade and becoming more diverse. This is not the overheated real estate market of New York City, but the city council has understood that a tax abatement intended to encourage redevelopment downtown has served its purpose and is now being exploited by developers. Philadelphia is growing.

"I'm a sociologist, not a policy maker," I say to my students, "that's what I'm teaching you to become!" That said, I see lessons in this research for urbanists generally. We should embrace the potential of historic preservation to revitalize and mitigate and engage it directly. Historic preservation is one of the primary urban policy tools available to us that leaves substantial control over process in the hands of the neighborhood residents most immediately affected. That should lead us to encourage communities to take advantage of it, particularly those historically underserved by preservation efforts.

Preservation as a policy tool is most relevant in older U.S. cities. That is less of a constraint than the concern with how to align its impact with the interests of renters in neighborhoods dominated by rental housing. Preservation has often disproportionately favored the interests of the wealthy, but we should not concede yet that is an inevitable characteristic. There is an opportunity to use preservation rules to help regulate the quality of more affordable, market rate housing and to build community among renters and homeowners on the basis of the built environment they share in common.

I hope readers will take away many things from this research. Foremost among them is the clear sense that part of the complication of living in contemporary U.S. cities is that we inhabit an enduring built environment. Whether we intentionally preserve it or not, most of us live among and in buildings built long ago. Historic preservation efforts focus our attention on that enduring built environment and articulate one version of the role of that stuff in our lives. More important for me than the preservationist perspective is the way that the process, the struggle, reveals these ongoing relationships.

Appendix

DATA, METHODS, AND MEASURES

This appendix includes a detailed explanation of my methods. The overarching theme is what I think of as "triangulation:" an effort to complement any kind of data with other kinds of data that will help situate it (whether reinforcing or disconfirming). This approach emerges from my deep sense that cities are too complex to be described using a single method, but many individually insufficient factors may ultimately enable a compelling account.

Research Questions

How does historic district designation affect neighborhoods in cities in the United States? Relatedly, how do historic preservation policies provide tools for managing neighborhood change? For whom? And how do they use them? I focus on historic district designation, sometimes called landmark district designation, because the scale of districts makes them the relevant preservation phenomena for neighborhoods, frequently encompassing significant fractions of neighborhoods or contiguous with organic neighborhood boundaries. It is conceivable that individual landmarks—individual historic buildings—affect the neighborhoods around them, but that effect would be harder to detect. Moreover, district designation rules usually emerge from some kind of collective process and shape the ways many homeowners use their property, locating them in the kind of mutually constituting tangle that indicates the complexity of real urban processes.

District designation, in its various forms, requires some kind of local involvement, and it can be used by urban actors as a tool for accomplishing specific goals. District designation itself is often initiated by residents and usually requires community assent. To the degree that preservation regulations require local input on proposed changes to the built environment, they become a mechanism for local control over change, at least in that respect. To the degree that preservation is incentivized, through tax credits, for example, district designation becomes a way of directing resources to neighborhoods with old buildings. Who takes advantage of which aspects of designation and in what circumstances becomes important for understanding district designation's effects—designation is not simply a top-down process in relation to neighborhoods, it requires reinforcement from the bottom up.

To address these questions, I have undertaken a number of related investigations. In Baltimore, where district designation is extensive and good demographic data about neighborhoods is available, I began by examining the relationship between district designation and neighborhood change quantitatively. I observe key neighborhood demographics—racial composition, household income, and educational attainment—before and after district designation and compare them with never-designated parts of the city. I also connect these data to the use of historic rehabilitation tax credits in Baltimore and to rates of housing vacancy. Similar, if less fine-grained, data were produced about New York City by NYU's Furman Center (Core-Data.nyc) that allows a basic comparison, or at least a similar observation of trends.

In Baltimore, I have also tried to address the second question—how preservation policy is used. I have done so by talking to leading preservationists, both within and outside city government, all of whom emphasize stabilization and revitalization in this shrinking or "legacy" city context. Preservation in Baltimore is dominated by two organizations, one governmental (Commission on Historic and Architectural Preservation [CHAP]) and one nonprofit (Baltimore Heritage), that owe their existence to the same founder and the same era. They seem to function in friendly, if sometimes critical relation to one another.

My historic tax credit data describes the primary mechanism by which preservation regulation is used to facilitate revitalization in Baltimore. I have tried to capture the perspective of residents pursuing district designation through a review of the Baltimore CHAP designation files, each of which chart the process from its earliest stages through city council's approval, including numerous struggles over boundaries and etcetera. I have also interviewed residents involved in preservation processes whenever possible.

Because preservation is not a unitary process, I have chosen a kind of "most different" cases approach. In contrast to Baltimore, I have taken up these same questions—giving primacy to the policy and strategy pieces—in central Brooklyn, a gentrifying part of a booming city. An old friend introduced me to a neighborhood preservation advocate in Prospect Heights, one of the primary local residents responsible for the designation of that neighborhood. The rest of my interview sample in New York City has followed his activist network outward to cover the nearby neighborhoods of Crown Heights North and South and Bedford-Stuyvesant, and the leadership of their preservation efforts. Neighborhood preservationists in New York seem to rely on one another for strategic support in their relationship with community boards, the Landmarks Preservation Commission, and the city council; thus, within a reasonable degree of geographic proximity, they all know each other. These clustered neighborhoods also confront similar conditions, if at different moments, and change within each is related to change in the others. I also included in this sample citywide figures such as the leader of the city's foremost preservation nonprofit, to whom many of my interviewees had referred. At times I have relied on published interviews or oral histories from leaders with whom I could not schedule interviews. All of this gives me a good window through which to look into how preservation activists in Brooklyn use preservation regulations to manage neighborhood change.

This approach does not make for a perfect comparison because I cannot provide the same kind of data for each city or part of a city in a way that would enable me to examine the same process in two different places. But that is because the same process does not take place in radically different cities (might not, in fact, be the same across any combination of cities). The point for me is to reveal that preservation—district designation in particular—is initiated and plays out differently depending on the specific details of the context of any particular effort. By selecting cases from roughly opposite ends of a spectrum of urban development dynamics and observing how designation operates in these cases, I can demonstrate that there is a wide range of preservation-related activity. If a few commonalities remain between Baltimore and Brooklyn, they are that much more interesting when detected across such radically contrasting contexts.

Baltimore Data

Baltimore, for reasons I do not yet fully understand (numerous educational institutions, long history of urban decline and revitalization efforts, perhaps), provides a remarkable opportunity for just the kind of analysis that my particular set of questions requires. The city has used historic district designation extensively, and historically designated districts of various types constitute a significant proportion of the city's real estate in many different neighborhoods. Baltimore CHAP has made a great deal of information about the city's historic districts easily available online, posting maps, descriptions, and dates of designation, broken down by type (national, state, city), and various organizations around the city (the Neighborhood Indicators Alliance-Jacob France Institute, the Department of Planning, Johns Hopkins University) have cooperated to make data about Baltimore's neighborhoods available to the public. This makes it easy to secure and analyze information about demographic changes in Baltimore historic districts across their designation and to compare this information with parts of the city that have not been designated. Baltimore provides an opportunity to examine the relationship between historic district designation and neighborhood change in depth, readily admitting that we should recognize the limits of a single city study.

Quantitative Approach

Of seventy-three historic districts (HDs) in Baltimore designated between 1969 and 2015, thirty are predominantly residential neighborhoods significantly coterminous with "neighborhood statistical areas" (NSAs), for which the city provided demographic data from 1980 through 2010. This allowed me to conduct straightforward analyses of change over time before or soon after designation and through the decades that followed. This fortuitous degree of matching is relatively rare in geographic studies and allows a greater confidence in the numbers than would be possible using Census block groups or tracts.

Having downloaded Census data from 1980, 1990, 2000, and 2010, broken down by NSA, and made available either by the Baltimore Department of Planning or by the Government Publications Library at Johns Hopkins University, I reconciled NSAs across the four years and eliminated nonresidential NSAs. Beginning from 267 NSAs in 1980, 312 in 1990, 241 in 2000, and 262 in 2010, I identified the 228 predominantly residential NSAs that were consistent across the period and for which I had data for at least three of the four possible data points. Using maps published by Baltimore's Planning Department and CHOP, I matched historic districts with the NSAs with which they overlapped.

I took a low-tech approach—matching NSAs and HDs by eye—that was facilitated by the form of these units of analysis. Both HDs and NSAs in Baltimore appear to follow organic neighborhood boundaries and thus frequently share boundaries, although any given HD may include multiple NSAs. I eliminated any HDs that were significantly smaller than the NSA within which they fell or did not match for other reasons. This left me with 59 NSAs that were ever within HDs and 168 NSAs never within an HD.

Across all four census years, the NSA data include total population, white population, Black population, bachelor's degree or greater for those twenty-five and older (BA-plus), high school degree, median household income, total housing units, and occupancy and vacancy. A few other variables show up in some years but not all. Because questions of gentrification drive the project, I calculated and focused on variables that would indicate status changes in neighborhood population, specifically percent White, percent BA-plus, and median household income. Baltimore is overwhelmingly Black and White, thus the percent White is usually the inverse of percent Black, although by 2010 approximately 5 percent of the population identified in some other racialized category. I also calculated the percent of units vacant in an NSA because of the potential relevance of vacancy for gentrification processes (at least in indicating the neighborhood's ability to accommodate new residents).

I identified NSAs within HDs by the year in which the district was designated according to the National Register of Historic Places because all of the HDs have this in common. My dated HDs were all designated (with one exception in 1998) in one of three periods: 1969–74, 1980–83, 2001–2004. This raises questions that will require further investigation. I later added data on a loose cluster of HDs designated from 2006 to 2015, but they are much more like the rest of the city.

These tight and distinct clusters encouraged me to examine the neighborhood demographic data. Clustering HD NSAs according to designation date allows me to examine trends in the kinds of neighborhoods that were designated historic in the three different periods and notice the differences among them. The cluster comparison and the trajectories of individual clusters also contributed to my consideration of the designation-gentrification relationship, although no definitive account emerged.

With matched-pair studies in mind (Sharkey's 2008 study made a big impression), I went further into my data to see if I could pair HD and never-designated NSAs with similar characteristics at baseline, then track their trajectories as another approach to estimating the impact of historic district designation. My three key characteristics (race, education, income) varied nearly independently in Baltimore neighborhoods, so the matching task seemed initially impossible—when I found NSAs that were similar in one way, they were different in another (an important observation in itself). Accordingly, I matched HDs and never-designated neighborhoods according to thresholds for one variable at a time. For example, I matched HD and never-designated NSAs that were greater than 90 percent white or less than 20 percent white in 1980, the top and bottom of the distribution. Similarly, I matched NSAs with more than 20 percent BA-plus in 1980 and NSAs with less than 10 percent BA-plus in 1980. For median household income, I created three tiers: NSAs greater than $20,000, between $10,000 and $20,000, and less than $10,000. The outcome of this set of observations suggests that HD NSAs are different from never-designated areas and that they change differently over time, at least in some respects.

Qualitative Approach

Various aspects of the quantitative data about Baltimore demanded further detail. Why, for example, was designation clustered into these three periods? For that matter, why were a handful of the districts designated in the week between Christmas and the new year? More important, how did preservationists conceive of the preservation project in Baltimore? Why was designation so extensive? Some of these questions resisted resolution, but others could be tackled through interviewing.

One of my Columbia urban studies majors had drawn heavily on the work of a Baltimore-based urbanist who turned out to be on CHAP (appointed citizen). She introduced me to CHAP's executive director, Eric Holcombe, and to Executive Director Johns Hopkins[1] of Baltimore Heritage, the preservation nonprofit founded by architect Bo Kelly in 1960, four years prior to his founding chairmanship of CHAP. They both proved to be willing and welcoming informants beyond any reasonable expectation. Holcombe gave me access to CHAP's designation files, which helped me understand the process. I conducted multiple interviews with both over the course of a few years, focused on the activities of their organizations and their understanding of preservation in Baltimore more generally. I also forged a relationship with Baltimore Heritage's director of preservation and outreach, Eli Pousson, sharing public data and discussing preservation-related processes in Baltimore.

CHAP's local district designation files enabled me to trace the process of and conflicts surrounding designation in Baltimore neighborhoods. I spent multiple days at CHAP's headquarters in the summer of 2016. I focused on large and prominent historic districts, beginning with the original correspondence initiating the process of designation. The files revealed intentions and motivations, resistance, and resolution, giving a clearer sense of the various reasons designation was pursued.

Brooklyn Data

My Brooklyn interview and observation sample emerged from a happy accident. An old, locally active friend, whose co-op apartment in Prospect Heights I'd long ago helped him move into (wondering at the time why anyone would do so), introduced me to Gib Veconi, then chair of the Prospect Heights Neighborhood Development Council (PHNDC), "the leading civic organization providing advocacy for neighborhood-wide issues on behalf of the residents and businesses of Prospect Heights."[2] Veconi led the landmark district designation effort in Prospect Heights, beginning in 2006, in response in major part to the Atlantic Yards project nearby (including the Barclays Center, home of the NBA's Brooklyn Nets, and 6,430 units of housing, planned). PHNDC's landmarks committee reviews proposed changes to buildings within the landmark district, makes recommendations to the local community board, and testifies before the New York City Landmarks Preservation Commission (LPC), thus functioning as the local regulator, given the general deference of the citywide agency to local claims.

Veconi connected me to many other central Brooklyn preservation advocates, among them Danae Oratowski, secretary of PHNDC at the time I spoke with her; Suzanne Spellen, columnist and historian for brownstoner.com, a member of the Crown Heights North Association, and one of the leaders of their landmark district designation process; Ethel Tyus, attorney and cofounder of the Crown Heights North Association; and Evelyn Tully Costa, designer, chair of the Crown Heights South Association, and leader of the ongoing district designation effort there. I reinforced my interviews with Spellen and Tyus by securing the New York Preservation Archive Project's oral history of the founding of the Crown Heights North Association in 2001 by Denise Brown-Puryear and Deborah Young and their involvement in preservation.[3]

These contacts led me to neighboring Bedford-Stuyvesant (Bed-Stuy), through realtor and preservation aficionado Morgan Munsey, and to the Community Board 3 (ad hoc) landmarks committee. I observed a number of landmarks committee meetings, in which proposals for changes to buildings within the local landmark district were evaluated for appropriateness. I then interviewed key members of the committee, Reno Dakota and Omar Walker. In the case of Bed-Stuy, I was again able to complement in-person interviews with published interviews of local advocates including Claudette Brady, who contributed to the expansion of the Stuyvesant Heights landmark district and led the designation of the Bedford Corners district.

Everyone I spoke to in Brooklyn told me I had to interview Simeon Bankoff, executive director of the Historic Districts Council, because he knew everyone and was either involved in or consulted about all landmarking efforts in the city. Bankoff described his nonprofit organization's relationship to New York City's LPC in similar terms to those Johns Hopkins used about the relationship of Baltimore Heritage to CHAP: "the loyal opposition." An accidental contact at a conference on preservation in legacy cities put me in touch with her former colleagues at LPC, giving me the opportunity to get a view from inside the workings of that bureaucracy. Another professional contact afforded me a kind of roundtable conversation with a number of employees of the New York Landmarks Conservancy, further helping me understanding the ecology of preservation in New York City.

NYU Furman Center Data

New York University's Furman Center studies real estate and development in New York City from a policy-relevant, social-scientific angle. They publish position papers on housing issues, such as whether preservation policies constrain development (2014). They also perform an important public service by collecting and publishing substantially descriptive data about the city. On the fiftieth anniversary of the historic preservation enabling legislation in New York City, the law that created the LPC, the

Furman Center published "Fifty Years of Historic Preservation in New York City" (2016). It contains extensive data comparing historic districts to the neighborhoods around them, throughout the city, but specifically including the neighborhoods of Brooklyn in which I am interested. Although not quite as fine-grained as my Baltimore data, their Brooklyn data is substantially comparable.

CONCLUSION

Some readers may resist the methodological diversity of my research. My understanding of what I have accomplished is the compelling and transparent presentation of accurate data, neutrally assembled and reported, that indicate the complexity of the urban phenomenon in question. These are true tales of Baltimore and Brooklyn. They are not the only possible findings about the relationship between preservation and neighborhood change in those cities, but the primary intention of my research is to suggest the potential to discern more and different aspects of this relationship. As Robert Sampson notes, when we undertake social scientific research on cities, we often find ourselves driven to portray processes separately that necessarily go together.[4] I have acknowledged that problem by taking a kaleidoscopic approach rather than one that artificially isolates features of urban processes from each other.

NOTES

1. INTRODUCTION

1. I capitalize White, because it is not the default American identity, not just "everyone else" or "normal people" or "us," but an identity with affirmative content (like Black) that is critically associated with access to diverse resources that preserve the privilege of White Americans, both historically and in the contemporary era.

2. Thomas F. Gieryn, "What Buildings Do," *Theory and Society* 31, no. 1 (2002): 35–74; Jeffrey L. Kidder, *Urban Flow: Bike Messengers and the City* (Ithaca, NY: Cornell University Press, 2012); Denise L. Lawrence and Setha M. Low, "The Built Environment and Spatial Form," *Annual Review of Anthropology* 19, no. 1 (1990): 453–505, https://doi.org/10.1146/annurev.an.19.100190.002321; Aaron Passell, *Building the New Urbanism: Places, Professions, and Profits in the American Metropolitan Landscape* (New York: Routledge, 2013).

3. Jane Jacobs, *The Death and Life of Great American Cities* (New York: Random House, 1961).

4. Suzanne Spellen, interview with author, April 6, 2016.

5. Edward Glaeser, "Preservation Follies: Excessive Landmarking Threatens to Make Manhattan a Refuge for the Rich," *City Journal* 20, no. 2 (2010), https://www.city-journal.org/html/preservation-follies-13279.html; Edward Glaeser, *Triumph of the City: How Urban Spaces Make Us Human* (Stuttgart: Pan Macmillan, 2011); Ingrid Gould Ellen, Brian McCabe, and Eric Stern, *Fifty Years of Historic Preservation in New York City* (New

York: NYU Furman Center, 2016), https://furmancenter.org/research /publication/fifty-years-of-historic-preservation-in-new-york-city228.

6. Stephanie Ryberg-Webster and Kelly L. Kinahan, "Historic Preservation in Declining City Neighbourhoods: Analysing Rehabilitation Tax Credit Investments in Six US Cities," *Urban Studies* 54, no. 7 (May 2017): 1673–91, https://doi.org/10.1177/0042098016629313; Stephanie Ryberg-Webster and Kelly L. Kinahan, "Historic Preservation and Urban Revitalization in the Twenty-First Century," *Journal of Planning Literature* 29, no. 2 (May 2014): 119–39, https://doi.org/10.1177/0885412213510524.

7. Ryberg-Webster and Kinahan, "Historic Preservation in Declining City Neighbourhoods"; Baltimore Commission on Historic and Architectural Preservation, "Tax Credits," accessed April 2, 2020, https://chap .baltimorecity.gov/tax-credits.

8. The rehabilitation tax credit is only available for maintenance costs associated with income-producing properties, thus not owner-occupied homes.

9. For more on the struggle to establish and define historic significance, see Melinda J. Milligan, "Buildings as History: The Place of Collective Memory in the Study of Historic Preservation," *Symbolic Interaction* 30, no. 1 (2007): 105–23.

10. Advisory Council on Historic Preservation, "Promoting Historic Preservation Across the Nation," accessed April 2, 2020, achp.gov; National Trust for Historic Preservation, "We're Saving Places," accessed April 2, 2020, savingplaces.org/we-are-saving-places; National Trust for Historic Preservation, "About Us," accessed October 5, 2011, preservationnation .org/about-us/history.html.

11. National Park Service, "Historic Preservation," accessed April 2, 2020, https://www.nps.gov/subjects/historicpreservation/index.htm.

12. National Register, Title 36, chap. 1, pt. 60, sec. 60.3.

13. National Trust for Historic Preservation, "Frequently Asked Questions About Historic Districts," accessed October 5, 2011, http://www.preservation nation.org/resources/faq/historic-districts/what-is-a-historic-district .html. The site has since been updated and the quote no longer appears (savingplaces.org/stories/eight-tips-for-understanding-the-complexities -of-historic-districts).

14. Patrick Hauck, interview with author, June 3, 2010.

15. Melissa Jest, interview with author, July 2, 2010.

16. Simeon Bankoff, interview with author, October 19, 2016.

17. Robert J. Sampson, *Great American City: Chicago and the Enduring Neighborhood Effect* (Chicago: University of Chicago Press, 2012).

18. David E. Clark and William E. Herrin, "Historical Preservation Districts and Home Sale Prices: Evidence from the Sacramento Housing Market," *Review of Regional Studies* 27, no. 1 (1997): 29–48; James R. Cohen, "Combining Historic Preservation and Income Class Integration: A Case Study of the Butchers Hill Neighborhood of Baltimore," *Housing Policy Debate* 9, no. 3 (January 1998): 663–97, https://doi.org /10.1080/10511482.1998.9521311; N. Edward Coulson and Michael L. Lahr, "Gracing the Land of Elvis and Beale Street: Historic Designation and Property Values in Memphis," *Real Estate Economics* 33, no. 3 (2005): 487–507, https://doi.org/10.1111/j.1540-6229.2005.00127.x; Edward Coulson and Robin M. Leichenko, "The Internal and External Impact of Historical Designation on Property Values," *Journal of Real Estate Finance and Economics* 23, no. 1 (July 2001): 113–24, https:// doi.org/10.1023/A:1011120908836; Deborah Ann Ford, "The Effect of Historic District Designation on Single-Family Home Prices," *Real Estate Economics* 17, no. 3 (1989): 353–62, https://doi.org/10.1111/1540 -6229.00496; Dennis E. Gale, "The Impacts of Historic District Designation Planning and Policy Implications," *Journal of the American Planning Association* 57, no. 3 (September 1991): 325–40, https://doi .org/10.1080/01944369108975503; Robin M. Leichenko, N. Edward Coulson, and David Listokin, "Historic Preservation and Residential Property Values: An Analysis of Texas Cities," *Urban Studies* 38, no. 11 (October 2001): 1973–87, https://doi.org/10.1080/00420980120080880; Andrew J. Narwold, "Estimating the Value of the Historical Designation Externality," *International Journal of Housing Markets and Analysis* 1, no. 3 (January 2008): 288–95, https://doi.org/10.1108/17538270810895123; Andrew Narwold, Jonathan Sandy, and Charles Tu, "Historic Designation and Residential Property Values," *International Real Estate Review* 11, no. 1 (February 2008): 83–95, https://www.um.edu.mo/fba//irer /papers/past/vol11n1_pdf/Article%204.pdf; Dan S. Rickman, "Neighborhood Historic Preservation Status and Housing Values in Oklahoma County, Oklahoma," *Journal of Regional Analysis and Policy* 39,

no. 2 (2009): 1–10, https://doi.org/10.22004/ag.econ.132429; Douglas S. Noonan, "Finding an Impact of Preservation Policies: Price Effects of Historic Landmarks on Attached Homes in Chicago, 1990–1999," *Economic Development Quarterly* 21, no. 1 (February 2007): 17–33, https:// doi.org/10.1177/0891242406296326.

19. Vicki Been, Ingrid Gould Ellen, Michael Gedal, Edward Glaeser, and Brian J. McCabe, "Preserving History or Restricting Development? The Heterogeneous Effects of Historic Districts on Local Housing Markets in New York City," *Journal of Urban Economics* 92 (March 2016): 16–30, https://doi.org/10.1016/j.jue.2015.12.002; David B. Fein, "Historic Districts: Preserving City Neighborhoods for the Privileged," *New York University Law Review* 60 (1985): 64–103; Glaeser, "Preservation Follies"; Glaeser, *Triumph of the City*; Michael deHaven Newsom, "Blacks and Historic Preservation," *Law and Contemporary Problems* 36 (1971): 423–31; David Wilson, "Making Historical Preservation in Chicago: Discourse and Spatiality in Neo-liberal Times," *Space and Polity* 8, no. 1 (April 2004): 43–59, https://doi.org/10.1080/1356257041000167884 2.

20. Philip Kasinitz, "The Gentrification of 'Boerum Hill': Neighborhood Change and Conflicts over Definitions," *Qualitative Sociology* 11, no. 3 (September 1988): 163–82, https://doi.org/10.1007/BF00988953; Cameron Logan, "Beyond a Boundary: Washington's Historic Districts and Their Racial Contents," *Urban History Review / Revue d'histoire Urbaine* 41, no. 1 (2012): 57–68, https://doi.org/10.7202/1013764ar.

21. Stephanie Ryberg-Webster and Kelly L. Kinahan, "Historic Preservation and Urban Revitalization in the Twenty-First Century," *Journal of Planning Literature* 29, no. 2 (May 2014): 119–39, https://doi .org/10.1177/0885412213510524.

22. NYU Furman Center, "CoreData.nyc," accessed April 2, 2020.

2. EXPLAINING CHANGE IN BALTIMORE'S HISTORIC NEIGHBORHOODS

1. N. Edward Coulson and Robin M. Leichenko, "Internal and External Impact of Historical Designation on Property Values," *Journal of Real Estate Finance and Economics* 23, no. 1 (July 2001): 113–24, https:// doi.org/10.1023/A:1011120908836; Dennis E. Gale, "Impacts of Historic

District Designation Planning and Policy Implications," *Journal of the American Planning Association* 57, no. 3 (September 1991): 325–40, https://doi.org/10.1080/01944369108975503; Andrew Narwold, Jonathan Sandy, and Charles Tu, "Historic Designation and Residential Property Values," *International Real Estate Review* 11 (February 2008): 83–95; Douglas S. Noonan, "Finding an Impact of Preservation Policies: Price Effects of Historic Landmarks on Attached Homes in Chicago, 1990–1999," *Economic Development Quarterly* 21, no. 1 (February 2007): 17–33, https://doi.org/10.1177/0891242406296326.

2. Philip Kasinitz, "The Gentrification of 'Boerum Hill': Neighborhood Change and Conflicts Over Definitions," *Qualitative Sociology* 11, no. 3 (September 1988): 163–82, https://doi.org/10.1007/BF00988953; Loretta Lees, Tom Slater, and Elvin Wyly, *Gentrification* (New York: Routledge, 2013); Cameron Logan, "Beyond a Boundary: Washington's Historic Districts and Their Racial Contents," *Urban History Review / Revue d'histoire Urbaine* 41, no. 1 (2012): 57–68, https://doi.org/10.7202/1013764ar.

3. Lei Ding, Jackelyn Hwang, and Eileen Divringi, "Gentrification and Residential Mobility in Philadelphia," *Regional Science and Urban Economics* 61 (November 2016): 38–51, https://doi.org/10.1016/j.regsciurbeco.2016.09.004; Nancy Holman and Gabriel M. Ahlfeldt, "No Escape? The Coordination Problem in Heritage Preservation," *Environment and Planning A: Economy and Space* 47, no. 1 (January 2015): 172–87, https://doi.org/10.1068/a130229p; Brian J. McCabe and Ingrid Gould Ellen, "Does Preservation Accelerate Neighborhood Change? Examining the Impact of Historic Preservation in New York City," *Journal of the American Planning Association* 82, no. 2 (April 2016): 134–46, https://doi.org/10.1080/01944363.2015.1126195; Suleiman Osman, *The Invention of Brownstone Brooklyn: Gentrification and the Search for Authenticity in Postwar New York* (New York: Oxford University Press, 2011); Kate S. Shaw and Iris W. Hagemans, " 'Gentrification Without Displacement' and the Consequent Loss of Place: The Effects of Class Transition on Low-Income Residents of Secure Housing in Gentrifying Areas," *International Journal of Urban and Regional Research* 39, no. 2 (2015): 323–41, https://doi.org/10.1111/1468-2427.12164.

4. "Baltimore, Maryland Population History 1840–2018," accessed July 25, 2018, www.biggestuscities.com/city/baltimore-maryland.

5. Roads to the Future, "Baltimore Early Expressway Planning," October 24, 1998, http://www.roadstothefuture.com/Balt_Early_Expwy_Plan.html.

6. Eric Holcomb, interview with author, July 13, 2016.

7. Evan McKenzie, *Privatopia: Homeowner Associations and the Rise of Residential Private Government* (New Haven, CT: Yale University Press, 1994).

8. Johns Hopkins, executive director, Baltimore Heritage, interview with author, July 13, 2016.

9. Historic districts in Baltimore are counted as National Register districts here, although many are both locally and nationally designated. National Register designation does not guarantee much control over the built environment for the local community, but it does grant access to the tax credit program.

10. Hopkins, interview. His name is, in fact, the same as that of the eponymous Baltimore university, to whose first benefactor he is distantly related.

11. The relationship between the Historic Districts Council and the New York City LPC is similar, according to Simeon Bankoff, executive director, Historic Districts Council, interview with author, October 19, 2016.

12. Personal correspondence with Johns Hopkins, December 15, 2016.

13. John R. Logan and Harvey Luskin Molotch, *Urban Fortunes: The Political Economy of Place* (Berkeley: University of California Press, 2007).

14. Kelly L. Kinahan, "Historic Preservation as a Community Development Tool in Legacy City Neighbourhoods," *Community Development Journal* 54, no. 4 (2019): 581–604.

15. MFI (median *family* income as reported in 1970) is comparable to MHI (median *household* income) thereafter.

16. Dollar figures are reproduced as they are reported, not adjusted.

17. Northwood did not match the tract it falls within, so I do not have 1970 data for it.

18. Robert J. Sampson, *Great American City: Chicago and the Enduring Neighborhood Effect* (Chicago: University of Chicago Press, 2012).

19. Lauren Schiszik, "Equity in Historic Preservation Planning in Baltimore," *Saving Places* (blog), February 23, 2017, http://forum.savingplaces.org/blogs/special-contributor/2017/02/23/equity-in-historic-preservation-planning-in-baltimore.

20. Baltimore City Commission on Historic and Architectural Preservation, "Baltimore City Tax Credit for Historic Restorations and Rehabilitations," accessed April 26, 2017, chap.baltimorecity.gov/tax-credits.

21. Holcomb, interview.

22. I could not secure similar data for this program.

23. Joseph Cronyn and Evans Paull, "Heritage Tax Credits: Maryland's Own Stimulus to Renovate Buildings for Productive Use and Create Jobs, an $8.53 Return on Every State Dollar Invested," *Abell Report* 22, no. 1 (March 2009): 1–8, https://www.abell.org/sites/default/files/publications/arn309.pdf.

24. The Maryland Sustainable Communities Tax Credit has had similar impact and faces similar constraints. See Melissa Archer, "Historic Rehabilitation Tax Credits," Maryland Department of Planning, Maryland Historical Trust, September 24, 2014.

25. Partnership for Building Reuse, "Partnership for Building Reuse: Building on Baltimore's History," *Baltimore Heritage*, 2014, https://baltimoreheritage.org/project/building-on-baltimore-history/.

26. See also Stephanie Ryberg-Webster and Kelly L Kinahan, "Historic Preservation in Declining City Neighbourhoods: Analysing Rehabilitation Tax Credit Investments in Six US Cities," *Urban Studies* 54, no. 7 (May 2017): 1673–91, https://doi.org/10.1177/0042098016629313.

27. The HTC has not been used in all Baltimore historic districts, thus the twenty-eight considered here are a subset of the fifty-five for which I have data.

28. I can provide an illustration of these geographic trends at the reader's request.

29. Robert J. Sampson, *Great American City: Chicago and the Enduring Neighborhood Effect* (Chicago: University of Chicago Press, 2012).

30. Richard Florida, *The Rise of the Creative Class* (New York: Basic, 2019).

31. The national average, for 1980, was 17 percent. United States Census Bureau, "Educational Attainment in the United States: 1981 & 1980 Tables," November 21, 2016, www.census.gov/data/tables/time-series/demo/educational-attainment/p20-390.html.

32. United States Census Bureau, "Educational Attainment in the United States: 2010," accessed July 14, 2017, www.census.gov/data/tables/2010/demo/educational-attainment/cps-detailed-tables.html.

33. See also George Galster and Jason Booza, "The Rise of the Bipolar Neighborhood," *Journal of the American Planning Association* 73, no. 4 (December 2007): 421–35, https://doi.org/10.1080/01944360708978523.

34. Brian J. McCabe and Ingrid Gould Ellen, "Does Preservation Accelerate Neighborhood Change? Examining the Impact of Historic Preservation in New York City," *Journal of the American Planning Association* 82, no. 2 (April 2016): 134–46, https://doi.org/10.1080/01944363.2015.112 6195.

3. MITIGATING GENTRIFICATION THROUGH PRESERVATION IN CENTRAL BROOKLYN

1. Saskia Sassen, *The Global City: New York, London, Tokyo* (Princeton, NJ: Princeton University Press, 1991).

2. Loretta Lees, Tom Slater, and Elvin Wyly, *Gentrification* (New York: Routledge, 2013).

3. Otis Pratt Pearsall, "The Reminiscences of Otis Pratt Pearsall," interviewed by Andrew Berman for the New York Preservation Archive Project, 2004, https://www.nypap.org/oral-history/otis-pratt-pearsall/.

4. Lees, Slater, and Wyly, *Gentrification*.

5. Philip Kasinitz, "The Gentrification of 'Boerum Hill': Neighborhood Change and Conflicts Over Definitions," *Qualitative Sociology* 11, no. 3 (September 1988): 163–82, https://doi.org/10.1007/BF00988953; Jonathan Lethem, *The Fortress of Solitude* (New York: Doubleday, 2003).

6. The only time I was actively threatened while doing this research, including extensive walking observation of neighborhoods in Baltimore and central Brooklyn, was returning to my car one evening after a community meeting in Bed-Stuy. Although anecdotal, this captured for me the heightened tensions in a neighborhood undergoing rapid transformation.

7. Pearsall, "The Reminiscences of Otis Pratt Pearsall."

8. Tenzing Chadotsang, interview with author, February 8, 2017.

9. The Landmarks Preservation Commission explains this stage in the following terms: "The agency assesses potentially meritorious properties in light of many factors, including agency priorities, the agency's policy of designating resources in all five boroughs, and the importance

of the resource in the context of similar and/or already designated resources." Landmarks Preservation Commission, Evaluation in Light of Commission Priorities and Other Considerations, accessed July 8, 2020, http://www1.nyc.gov/site/lpc/designations/designations.page.

10. Chadotsang, interview. Note that Chadotsang does not use the term "gentrification." Also, this fits precisely with Suzanne Spellen's account of landmarking in Crown Heights North.

11. Claudette Brady, "Bedford Stuyvesant; Bedford Corners Historic District (proposed)," Historic Districts Council interview by Susan Hopper, October 20, 2010, http://hdc.org/neighborhood-partners/interview -claudette-brady-bedford-stuyvesant-bedford-corners.

12. Chadotsang, interview.

13. Chadotsang, interview. East New York is one of the last substantially low-income, overwhelmingly Black neighborhoods in Brooklyn, but it also is subject to Mayor Bill de Blasio's rezoning process in the interest of building more affordable housing.

14. Simeon Bankoff, interview with author, October 19, 2016.

15. Bankoff, interview.

16. Bankoff, interview. This aspect of preservation efforts is prominent in Glaeser's indictment of preservation and its relationship to housing affordability. See Edward Glaeser, "Preservation Follies: Excessive Landmarking Threatens to Make Manhattan a Refuge for the Rich," *City Journal* 20, no. 2 (2010); Edward Glaeser, *Triumph of the City: How Urban Spaces Make Us Human* (New York: Penguin, 2011).

17. Bankoff, interview. This is a reference, of course, to Supreme Court Justice Potter Stewart's famous formulation—"But I know it when I see it"—in his 1964 concurrence in *Jacobellis v. Ohio*, in which the Court reversed the indecency conviction of a cinema manager for showing Louis Malle's "Les Amants" [The Lovers]. This phrase has taken on a life of its own, so interpreting precisely how Bankoff intends it is difficult.

18. Mary Shuford, interview with author, April 13, 2016.

19. Suleiman Osman, *Invention of Brownstone Brooklyn: Gentrification and the Search for Authenticity in Postwar New York* (New York: Oxford University Press, 2011).

20. When I talked with Shuford in April 2016, Sterling Place across Washington Avenue (just outside the landmark district) showed evidence of

very recent and rapid high-end development in the form of multiple luxury apartment buildings.

21. Gib Veconi, interview with author, March 30, 2016.

22. Danae Oratowski, interview with author, April 20, 2016.

23. Jane Jacobs, *The Death and Life of Great American Cities* (New York: Random House, 1961).

24. See Steven D. Levitt, "Understanding Why Crime Fell in the 1990s: Four Factors That Explain the Decline and Six That Do Not," *Journal of Economic Perspectives* 18, no. 1 (March 2004): 163–90, https://doi .org/10.1257/0895330004773563485; and Patrick Sharkey, *Uneasy Peace: The Great Crime Decline, the Renewal of City Life, and the Next War on Violence* (New York: Norton, 2018).

25. NYU Furman Center, "CoreData.nyc User Guide," accessed April 2, 2020, https://furmancenter.org/coredata/userguide.

26. Ingrid Gould Ellen, Keren Mertens Horn, and Davin Reed, "Has Falling Crime Invited Gentrification," U.S. Center for Economic Studies Paper No. CES-WP-17-27, March 1, 2017, 36, https://dx.doi.org/10.2139 /ssrn.2930242.

27. The Crown Heights North historic district was designated in 2007, Crown Heights North II in 2011, Crown Heights North III in 2015, and the fourth phase is "in the planning stage." See Crown Heights North Association, "Landmark Phases," accessed July 27, 2018, www.crown heightsnorth.org/phase-map.html.

28. Denise Brown-Puryear and Deborah Young, "Saving Preservation Stories: Reminiscences of Denise Brown-Puryear & Deborah Young," interviewed by Liz H. Strong, August 17, 2015, www.nypap.org /oral-history/denise-brown-puryear-deborah-young/.

29. Suzanne Spellen, interview with author, April 6, 2016. I also interviewed Ethel Tyus, November 14, 2018, the Crown Heights North homeowner and attorney who worked with Brown-Puryear and Young to formalize the Crown Heights North Association.

30. Brown-Puryear and Young, "Saving Preservation Stories," 5, 2–3.

31. This relates also to Veconi's "democracy," and I will return to this in my conclusion.

32. Brown-Puryear and Young, "Saving Preservation Stories," 23.

33. This also harks back to Melissa Jest's point, in my introduction, that preservation in communities of color has to acknowledge broader systemic issues as well.

34. Brown-Puryear and Young, "Saving Preservation Stories," 47.

35. Suzanne Spellen, interview.

36. Brown-Puryear and Young, "Saving Preservation Stories," 17.

37. Brown-Puryear and Young, "Saving Preservation Stories," 28, 56, 66.

38. Spellen, interview.

39. Brown-Puryear and Young, "Saving Preservation Stories," 38–39, 30.

40. Brown-Puryear and Young, "Saving Preservation Stories," 39, 38.

41. After years of neglect and numerous false starts, the house was finally restored in 2018. See Cate Corcoran, "After Long Struggle, Crown Heights Antebellum Jewel Susan B. Elkins House Restored at Last," March 22, 2018, https://www.brownstoner.com/architecture/brooklyn -landmark-crown-heights-susan-elkins-house-1375-dean-street-amber -mazor/.

42. Brown-Puryear and Young, "Saving Preservation Stories," 55.

43. Spellen, interview. In fact, this raises a question about middle-class Black gentrification. Spellen also suggests that there were some newer, white homeowners involved in the landmarking process, people whose role in the neighborhood was much more like Veconi's and Oratowski's.

44. Spellen, interview.

45. I did not include Brooklyn as a whole in this chart because the borough is, overall, much less Black than these neighborhoods, declining from 34.2 percent Black in 2005 to 31.1 percent in 2014, and Brooklyn's inclusion would have compressed this chart.

46. See, for example, the work of noted film director Spike Lee.

47. CoreData.nyc, from which I have collected these data, does not provide subborough-level numbers further back than 2005.

48. Robert J. Sampson, *Great American City: Chicago and the Enduring Neighborhood Effect* (Chicago: University of Chicago Press, 2012), 107, 99.

49. Michael D. M. Bader and Maria Krysan, "Community Attraction and Avoidance in Chicago: What's Race Got to Do with It?," *The ANNALS of the American Academy of Political and Social Science* 660, no. 1 (July 2015): 261–81, https://doi.org/10.1177/0002716215577615.

50. Veconi, interview.

51. Reno Dakota, interview with author, May 26, 2016. The value Dakota places on aesthetics is confirmed by a published profile of his home emphasizing Dakota's painstaking decoration of their 1895 brownstone with period accuracy. See Steven Kurutz, "In Brooklyn, a Strict Victorian Brownstone," *New York Times*, July 26, 2012, www.nytimes.

com/2012/07/26/greathomesanddestinations/in-brooklyn-a-strict-victorian-brownstone-on-location.html.

52. Bed-Stuy is protected by the Stuyvesant Heights district, which was substantially expanded in 2013. The Bedford district was designated in 2015 and there are plans for Stuyvesant North and East districts.

53. Omar Walker, interview with author, June 13, 2016.

54. U.S. Census Bureau, "American Fact Finder," American Community Survey data.

55. Changes to the costs of living in a neighborhood that are associated with changes in local amenities, such as grocery stores and restaurants, have another, more indirect impact on homeowners.

56. NYC Department of Finance, "Property Tax Rates," accessed August 8, 2017, http://www1.nyc.gov/site/finance/taxes/property-tax-rates.page.

57. It may seem conspicuous that I have not dealt with household income here except to factor it into housing affordability. I chose to focus on other quantitative data because the income data for these neighborhoods are extremely volatile and do not indicate any particular trend during this time.

4. VACANCY, ABANDONMENT, DEMOLITION BY NEGLECT, AND PROJECT CORE IN BALTIMORE

1. "Baltimore's population stood at 611,648 as of July 1, 2017, according to new estimates from the U.S. Census Bureau. . . . Baltimore's population peaked after World War II, reaching almost 950,000 in 1950," declining 36 percent by 2017. Ian Duncan, "Baltimore Population Decline Continues, Census Estimates Show," *Baltimore Sun*, March 22, 2018.

2. See, for example, Advisory Council on Historic Preservation, "Managing Change: Preservation and Rightsizing in America," March 1, 2014, https://www.achp.gov/digital-library-section-106-landing/managing-change-preservation-and-rightsizing-america-0.

3. Eric Holcomb, interview with author, February 19, 2019.

4. James R. Cohen, "Abandoned Housing: Exploring Lessons from Baltimore," *Housing Policy Debate* 12, no. 3 (January 2001): 415–48, at 415, https://doi.org/10.1080/10511482.2001.9521413.

5. Cohen, "Abandoned Housing," 416, 429, 430.

6. Dennis P. Culhane and Amy E. Hillier, "Comment on James R. Cohen's 'Abandoned Housing: Exploring Lessons from Baltimore,'" *Housing Policy Debate* 12, no. 3 (January 2001): 449–55, https://doi.org/10.1080/10 511482.2001.9521414.

7. City of Detroit, "Detroit City's Demolition Program Information," accessed June 26, 2020, https://detroitmi.gov/departments/detroit-building -authority/detroit-demolition-program.

8. Luke Wenger and Yvonne Broadwater, "Gov. Hogan Announces $700M Plan to Target Urban Decay in Baltimore," *Baltimore Sun*, January 5, 2016.

9. Alan Mallach, "Laying the Groundwork for Change: Demolition, Urban Strategy, and Policy Reform," Brookings, September 24, 2012, https://www.brookings.edu/research/laying-the-groundwork-for -change-demolition-urban-strategy-and-policy-reform/.

10. Jason Hackworth, "Demolition as Urban Policy in the American Rust Belt," *Environment and Planning A: Economy and Space* 48, no. 11 (November 2016): 2201–22, https://doi.org/10.1177/0308518X16654914.

11. Jason Hackworth, "Race and the Production of Extreme Land Abandonment in the American Rust Belt," *International Journal of Urban and Regional Research* 42, no. 1 (2018): 51–73, https://doi.org /10.1111/1468-2427.12588.

12. Alan Mallach, "The Empty House Next Door: Understanding and Reducing Vacancy and Hypervacancy in the United States," Lincoln Institute of Land Policy, 2018, https://www.lincolninst.edu/sites /default/files/pubfiles/empty-house-next-door-full.pdf.

13. Lionel Foster, "'The Black Butterfly:' Racial Segregation and Investment Patterns in Baltimore," Urban Institute, February 5, 2019, https://apps .urban.org/features/baltimore-investment-flows/; Lawrence Brown, "Two Baltimores: The White L vs. the Black Butterfly," *Baltimore Sun*, June 28, 2016.

14. See, for example, "Baltimore Housing Market Typology," jointly developed by the Baltimore City Planning Department, Department of Housing & Community Development, and Reinvestment Fund, accessed April 10, 2020, https://planning.baltimorecity.gov/maps-data /housing-market-typology.

15. "Project C.O.R.E. FY17 Q4 Quarterly Report," Maryland Department of Housing and Community Development, June 2017, https://dhcd.maryland.gov/ProjectCORE/Documents/CORE_Quarterly Report_FY17_Q4.pdf.

16. Kacy Rohn, "Rebuilding Baltimore, From Urban Renewal to Project C.O.R.E.: Neighborhood Revitalization, Historic Preservation, and the Lessons of the Past" (master's thesis, University of Maryland, 2017), http://drum.lib.umd.edu/handle/1903/20543.

17. Editorial, "Hogan's Budget and Baltimore," *Baltimore Sun*, January 25, 2016; see also Matt Hill, Chris Lafferty, and Ty Hullinger, "The Reality of Gov. Hogan's Baltimore Investment," *Baltimore Sun*, January 17, 2016.

18. Rohn, "Rebuilding Baltimore," 59.

19. Rohn, "Rebuilding Baltimore," 64.

20. Rohn, "Rebuilding Baltimore," 68.

21. Rohn, "Rebuilding Baltimore," 75.

22. Ian Duncan, "$75M Plan to Demolish Thousands of Baltimore's Vacant Houses Now Relies on Other Groups, New Accounting," *Baltimore Sun*, October 26, 2017.

23. Rohn, "Rebuilding Baltimore," 80.

24. Office of Governor Larry Hogan, "Governor Larry Hogan Announces Latest Phase of Project C.O.R.E. Initiative" (press release), March 27, 2018, https://governor.maryland.gov/2018/03/27/governor-larry-hogan-announces-latest-phase-of-project-c-o-r-e-initiative/.

25. Eric Holcomb, interview with author, February 19, 2019.

26. Johns Hopkins, interview with author, July 11, 2018.

27. Holcomb, interview.

28. Hopkins, interview.

29. Holcomb, interview.

30. Open Baltimore, "Vacant Buildings," City of Baltimore, accessed May 14, 2019, https://data.baltimorecity.gov/Housing-Development/Vacant-Buildings/qqcv-ihn5.

31. See Cohen, "Abandoned Housing."

32. Andrea Merrill Goldwyn, "Demolition by Neglect: A Loophole in Preservation Policy" (master's thesis, University of Pennsylvania, 1995), https://repository.upenn.edu/hp_theses/357/; Rachel Ann Hildebrandt, "Demolition-By-Neglect: Where Are We Now?" (master's

thesis, University of Pennsylvania, 2012), https://repository.upenn.edu
/hp_theses/189/; Galen Newman and Jesse Saginor, "Four Imperatives
for Preventing Demolition by Neglect," *Journal of Urban Design* 19, no. 5
(October 20, 2014): 622–37, https://doi.org/10.1080/13574809.2014.94370
5; John M. Weiss, "Protecting Landmarks from Demolition by Neglect:
New York City's Experience," *Widener Law Review* 18 (2012): 309.

33. To put this in perspective, at the time of this writing, Catherine Pugh
had recently resigned as mayor and was sentenced to three years in
prison when evidence emerged of her efforts to enrich herself through
city contracts. Luke Broadwater, Justin Fenton, and Kevin Rector,
"Former Baltimore Mayor Catherine Pugh Sentenced to 3 Years for
'Healthy Holly' Children's Book Fraud Scheme," *Baltimore Sun*, February 27, 2020.

34. Joanne Whitely, *Hearing on Demolition by Neglect in Union Square,
before the Baltimore Commission on Historic and Architectural Preservation*, August 10, 1990, 3–7, 11, 16.

35. Maryellen Cahill, *Hearing on Demolition by Neglect in Union Square,
before the Baltimore Commission on Historic and Architectural Preservation*, August 10, 1990, 8.

36. Ardabella Fox, *Hearing on Demolition by Neglect in Union Square, before
the Baltimore Commission on Historic and Architectural Preservation*,
August 10, 1990, 16, 13.

37. A lien is a sum attached to the deed of a property that must be repaid,
in this case to the city for stabilization or demolitions costs, when the
property is sold. The lien mechanism is obviously a more effective way
to secure returns to the city when properties are likely to sell and for
significantly more than the value of the lien when they do. A lien has
the benefit of requiring minimal action on the part of the government
agency imposing it.

38. Fox, *Hearing on Demolition*, 13.

39. Cahill, *Hearing on Demolition*, 19.

40. John Huppert, *Hearing on Demolition by Neglect in Union Square, before
the Baltimore Commission on Historic and Architectural Preservation*,
August 10, 1990, 14, 17–19, 25.

41. Cahill, *Hearing on Demolition*, 19.

42. Huppert, *Hearing on Demolition*, 20–22, 25–26.

43. Cahill, *Hearing on Demolition*, 30.

44. Huppert, *Hearing on Demolition*, 31.

45. Ron Miles, *Hearing on Demolition by Neglect in Union Square, before the Baltimore Commission on Historic and Architectural Preservation*, August 10, 1990, 32.

46. "The Community Development Block Grant (CDBG) program is a flexible program that provides communities with resources to address a wide range of unique community development needs. Beginning in 1974, the CDBG program is one of the longest continuously run programs at HUD. The CDBG program provides annual grants on a formula basis to 1209 general units of local government and States." Housing and Urban Development, "Community Development Program," accessed October 2, 2019, https://www.hud.gov/program_offices /comm_planning/communitydevelopment/programs.

47. Miles, *Hearing on Demolition*, 32, 33–34.

48. Deborah Goodman, *Hearing on Demolition by Neglect in Union Square, before the Baltimore Commission on Historic and Architectural Preservation*, August 10, 1990, 11, 26.

49. David Norman, *Hearing on Demolition by Neglect in Union Square, before the Baltimore Commission on Historic and Architectural Preservation*, August 10, 1990, 12, 26.

50. Goodman and Norman, *Hearing on Demolition*, 40–41.

51. See also Cohen, "Abandoned Housing," 425, on Mayor Schmoke's ignoring city's shrinking, for another example of the impact of this attitude.

52. See Neil Smith, *The New Urban Frontier: Gentrification and the Revanchist City* (New York: Routledge, 2005), https://doi.org/10.4324 /9780203975640; Loretta Lees, Tom Slater, and Elvin Wyly, chap. 2 in *Gentrification* (New York: Routledge, 2013).

53. Richard Casey Sadler and Don J. Lafreniere, "Racist Housing Practices as a Precursor to Uneven Neighborhood Change in a Post-Industrial City," *Housing Studies* 32, no. 2 (2017): 186–208.

5. STRUGGLING TO PRESERVE IN THE CONTEXT OF AGGRESSIVE DEVELOPMENT PRESSURE

1. This committee is ad hoc, pointing to the rapidity with which neighborhood residents have felt they must respond to rapidly increasing pressure.

2. Dixon Leasing (website), accessed July 30, 2019, www.dixonleasing .com.

3. Rob Witherwax, interview with author, October 16, 2018.

4. A number of my Brooklyn interviewees acknowledged in our conversations that land use zoning could accomplish similar ends to those they are attempting to accomplish with landmarking, but they also argued that it was a much more intense process, more likely to encounter resistance, and less likely to succeed.

5. Witherwax, interview.

6. Ethel Tyus, interview with author, November 14, 2018.

7. Community Board 3, Landmarks Committee meeting, May 9, 2016. Suzanne Spellen connected me to Muncey, with whom she gives tours of historic Bedford-Stuyvesant, and he showed me around the neighborhood before spontaneously offering to bring me with him to the meeting.

8. Restoration Plaza (website), "About Us," accessed October 23, 2019, https://restorationplaza.org/about-us/.

9. Dun & Bradstreet, "Brookland Capital LLC Company Profile," accessed December 11, 2017, https://www.dnb.com/business-directory /company-profiles.brookland_capital_llc.4adffd1beco3ca40f771bf54ad2 1e7ea.html.

10. Camille Bautista, "Proposed Halsey Street Apt. Design Clashes with Historic Zone, Locals Say," March 19, 2017, www.dnainfo.com/new -york/20170317/bed-stuy/524-540-halsey-st-brookland-capital-bedford -stuyvesant-historic-district-condos-brooklyn.

11. Dixon Advisory USA is the manager of the U.S. Masters Residential Property Fund (U.S. Masters), a residential real estate investment trust (REIT) operating in the New York metropolitan area. U.S. Masters is focused on acquiring single-family houses (up to four dwellings) for acquisition, renovation, and rental. Dixon Advisory (website), accessed December 4, 2017, www.dixonadvisoryusa.com.

12. Evans Dixon, "About Us," accessed October 26, 2019, www.evansdixon .com.au/about-us.

13. Community Board 3, Landmarks Committee Meeting, May 9, 2016.

14. Community Board 3, Landmarks Committee Meeting, June 13, 2016.

15. Historic buildings in disinvested neighborhoods are often converted to single-room occupancy, both to provide inexpensive housing and to increase rates of profit for their owners.

16. Evelyn Tully Costa, interview with author, April 19, 2016.

17. Evelyn Tully Costa, interview with author, February 28, 2017.

18. Tully Costa, interviews, 2016 and 2017.

19. Tyus, interview. Ethel Tyus, a Crown Heights North resident instrumental in landmarking the Crown Heights North district, does not believe the Crown Heights South landmarking process will work until the differences between the longtime African American and Caribbean residents, newer white residents, and Lubavitchers can be worked out.

20. Tully Costa, interviews, 2016 and 2017.

21. I reviewed all of the local Brooklyn press available online for coverage of the process of its announcement, planning, and permitting and the resistance to that process. These sources are extensive, including *BKLYNER*, *Brooklyn Reader*, *Brooklyn Paper*, *Brownstoner*, *Curbed*, *DNAInfo*, *Gothamist*, and *Kings County Politics*, foremost, in addition to larger circulation publications like the *New York Daily News*, *The Guardian*, and *Politico*. New York City Economic Development Corporation also published press releases, state offices published reports, and the eventual developer of the armory, BFC Partners, produced a quarterly newsletter beginning in late 2016. Notable local bloggers such as "The Q at Parkside" provided further perspective.

22. New York State Department of Environmental Conservation, "Fact Sheet: Brownfield Cleanup Program, Bedford Union Armory," October 2018, http://www.dec.ny.gov/data/der/factsheet/c224252cuprop.pdf.

23. NYCEDC, "Vacant, Century-Old Armory on Bedford Avenue to Be Redeveloped Into Commercial and Residential Facility" (press release), December 17, 2015, https://www.nycedc.com/press-release/nycedc-president-torres-springer-borough-president-adams-council-member-cumbo-and.

24. Tully Costa, interview, 2017.

25. Megan Carpentier, "Brooklyn Lawmakers Enter Gentrification Feud Over Crown Heights Neighborhood." *The Guardian*, October 19, 2016.

26. Rachel Holliday Smith, "Brooklyn Armory Deal, and Larger De Blasio Development Debate, Move Toward Term Two," *Gotham Gazette*, December 11, 2017.

27. Tully Costa, interview, 2017.

28. Gaby Del Valle, "Crown Heights Residents Protest Development at Bedford-Union Armory," *Gothamist*, March 8, 2017.

29. Ameena Walker, "Crown Heights Residents of Color Won't Benefit from Bedford-Union Armory Project: Study," *Curbed NY*, March 25, 2017.

30. Rachel Sugar, "Bedford-Union Armory Developers Promise Union Jobs, Training Programs." *Curbed NY*, April 10, 2017.

31. Gloria Pazmino and Sally Goldenberg, "Cumbo to Oppose Bedford Armory Project, After Hesitating for Months," *Politico PRO*, May 18, 2017.

32. Tanay Warerkar, "Controversial Bedford-Union Armory Redevelopment Loses Cumbo's Support," *Curbed NY*, May 18, 2017.

33. Amy Plitt, "Protestors Came Out En Masse at Meeting to Discuss Pfizer, Bedford-Union Armory Developments," *Curbed NY*, July 11, 2017; Tanay Warerkar, "Bedford-Union Armory Redevelopment Unanimously Rejected by Community Board," *Curbed NY*, June 28, 2017.

34. Plitt, "Protestors Came Out En Masse at Meeting to Discuss Pfizer, Bedford-Union Armory Developments."

35. Amy Plitt, "Borough President Calls for 100 Percent Affordable Housing at Bedford-Union Armory Redevelopment." *Curbed NY*, September 2, 2017.

36. Sarah Amar, "Bedford-Union Armory Developer Faces Questions from City Planning Commission," *Gothamist*, September 20, 2017.

37. Pazmino and Goldenberg, "Cumbo to Oppose."

38. Tanay Warerkar, "Embattled Bedford-Union Armory Conversion Clears City Planning Commission," *Curbed NY*, October 30, 2017.

39. Brooklyn Reader, "Cumbo Announces Dramatically Modified Agreement for Bedford-Union," *BK Reader* (blog), November 22, 2017, https://www.bkreader.com/2017/11/22/cumbo-announces-dramatically -modified-agreement-bedford-union-armory/.

40. Colin Mixson, "Armed with a New Backer: Crown Heights Pol Declares Newfound Support for City's Armory Scheme Before Council," *Brooklyn Paper*, November 22, 2017.

41. Smith, "Brooklyn Armory Deal."

42. Colin Mixson, "No Aid: Judge Quashes Legal Aid Suit to Halt Bedford-Union Armory Development," *Brooklyn Paper*, July 30, 2018.

43. "Two Experts Debate Over the Bedford-Union Armory, Caveh Zahedi and BRIC TV Go To Sundance" (Video), *112BK*, accessed April 3, 2020, https://www.youtube.com/watch?v=LHXQLRoKgBM.

44. Mixson, "No Aid."

45. Tanay Warerkar, "Bedford-Union Armory Revamp Moves Forward with Plans for 15-Story Rental," *Curbed NY*, March 14, 2018.

46. Craig Hubert, "Second Rental Building at Bedford-Union Armory Redevelopment Will Be Eight Stories with 60 Units," *Brownstoner*, June 15, 2018.

47. Hubert, "Second Rental Building"; Colin Mixson, "Forward March: Builder Files Plans for New Tower at C'Heights Armory Amidst Ongoing Suit Against Project," *Brooklyn Paper*, June 20, 2018.

48. Warerkar, "Bedford-Union Armory Revamp Moves Forward."

49. Hubert, "Second Rental Building."

50. Tanay Warerkar, "Bedford-Union Armory's Community Center Gets $15M from Cuomo," *Curbed NY*, September 4, 2018. The J'ouvert celebrations are variously described as "Brooklyn's largest street party" and a parade marking the first day of Carnival, first celebrated by freed African Americans after Emancipation, but also drawing on Caribbean traditions.

51. Kelly Mena, "Cumbo Announces Bedford Union Armory Advisory Committee,"*KingsCountyPolitics*,April15,2019,https://www.kingscounty politics.com/cumbo-announces-bedford-union-armory-advisory -committee/.

52. Witherwax, interview.

6. CONCLUSION

1. Marvin "Doc" Cheatham, interview with author, July 26, 2019.

2. Daniel Rodenburg, interview with author, July 12, 2019.

3. Stephanie Ryberg-Webster and Kelly L Kinahan, "Historic Preservation in Declining City Neighbourhoods: Analysing Rehabilitation Tax Credit Investments in Six US Cities," *Urban Studies* 54, no. 7 (May 2017): 1673–91, https://doi.org/10.1177/0042098016629313.

4. Jason Hackworth, "Demolition as Urban Policy in the American Rust Belt," *Environment and Planning A: Economy and Space* 48, no. 11 (November 2016): 2201–22, https://doi.org/10.1177/0308518X16654914.

5. Denise Brown-Puryear and Deborah Young, "Saving Preservation Stories: Reminiscences of Denise Brown-Puryear & Deborah Young," interviewed by Liz H. Strong, August 17, 2015, 30, www.nypap.org/oral -history/denise-brown-puryear-deborah-young/.

6. David Harvey, "The New Urbanism and the Communitarian Trap," *Harvard Design Magazine* 1, no. 2 (1997); Thomas J. Sugrue, *The Origins*

of the Urban Crisis: Race and Inequality in Postwar Detroit (Princeton, NJ: Princeton University Press, 2014).

7. See, for example, Kelly L. Kinahan, "The Neighborhood Effects of Federal Historic Tax Credits in Six Legacy Cities," *Housing Policy Debate* 29, no. 1 (2019): 166–80; Ted Grevstad-Nordbrock and Igor Vojnovic, "Heritage-Fueled Gentrification: A Cautionary Tale from Chicago," *Journal of Cultural Heritage* 38 (2019): 261–70.

APPENDIX: DATA, METHODS, AND MEASURES

1. The scholar who connected me to him introduced him by saying, "his name is, believe it or not. . . ."

2. Prospect Heights Neighborhood Development Council (website), accessed January 30, 2017, phndc.org.

3. New York Preservation Archive Project, "Oral History Project," accessed, October 11, 2019, nypap.org/oral-history.

4. Robert J. Sampson, *Great American City: Chicago and the Enduring Neighborhood Effect* (Chicago: University of Chicago Press, 2012).

BIBLIOGRAPHY

Advisory Council on Historic Preservation. *Managing Change: Preservation and Rightsizing America.* March 1, 2014. https://www.achp.gov/digital-library -section-106-landing/managing-change-preservation-and-rightsizing -america-0.

———. "Notice of Proposed Policy Statement on Historic Preservation and Community Revitalization." *Federal Register,* March 3, 2016.

Ahlfeldt, Gabriel M., and Wolfgang Maennig. "Substitutability and Complementarity of Urban Amenities: External Effects of Built Heritage in Berlin." *Real Estate Economics* 38, no. 2 (2010): 285–323.

Amar, Sarah. "Bedford-Union Armory Developer Faces Questions From City Planning Commission." *Gothamist,* September 20, 2017.

Avrami, Erica. "Making Historic Preservation Sustainable." *Journal of the American Planning Association* 82, no. 2 (2016): 104–12.

Bader, Michael D. M., and Maria Krysan. "Community Attraction and Avoidance in Chicago: What's Race Got to Do with It?" *The ANNALS of the American Academy of Political and Social Science* 660, no. 1 (2015): 261–81.

Barthel, Diane. "Historic Preservation: A Comparative Analyses." *Sociological Forum* 4, no. 1 (1989): 87–105.

Been, Vicki, Ingrid Gould Ellen, Michael Gedal, Edward Glaeser, and Brian McCabe. *Preserving History or Hindering Growth? The Heterogeneous Effects of Historic Districts on Local Housing Markets in New York City.* Cambridge, MA: National Bureau of Economic Research, 2014.

———. "Preserving History or Restricting Development? The Heterogeneous Effects of Historic Districts on Local Housing Markets in New York City." *Journal of Urban Economics* 92 (2016): 16–30.

Brooklyn Reader. "Cumbo Announces Dramatically Modified Agreement for Bedford-Union . . ." *BK Reader*, November 11, 2017.

Brown, Lawrence. "Two Baltimores: The White L vs. the Black Butterfly." *Baltimore Sun*, June 28, 2016.

Brown-Saracino, Japonica. "Social Preservationists and the Quest for Authentic Community." *City & Community* 3, no. 2 (2004): 135–56.

——. *A Neighborhood That Never Changes: Gentrification, Social Preservation, and the Search for Authenticity.* Chicago: University of Chicago Press, 2010.

Building on Baltimore's History: The Partnership for Building Reuse. Preservation Green Lab and Urban Land Institute Baltimore, November 2014.

Byrne, J. Peter. "Historic Preservation and Its Cultured Despisers: Reflections on the Contemporary Role of Preservation Law in Urban Development." *George Mason Law Review* 19 (2011): 665.

Clark, David E., and William E. Herrin. "Historical Preservation Districts and Home Sale Prices: Evidence from the Sacramento Housing Market." *Review of Regional Studies; New Brunswick* 27, no. 1 (1997): 29–48.

Cohen, James R. "Combining Historic Preservation and Income Class Integration: A Case Study of the Butchers Hill Neighborhood of Baltimore." *Housing Policy Debate* 9, no. 3 (1998): 663–97.

——. "Abandoned Housing: Exploring Lessons from Baltimore." *Housing Policy Debate* 12, no. 3 (2001): 415–48.

Coulson, N. Edward, and Michael L. Lahr. "Gracing the Land of Elvis and Beale Street: Historic Designation and Property Values in Memphis." *Real Estate Economics* 33, no. 3 (2005): 487–507.

Coulson, N. Edward, and Robin M. Leichenko. "The Internal and External Impact of Historical Designation on Property Values." *Journal of Real Estate Finance and Economics* 23, no. 1 (2001): 113–24.

——. "Historic Preservation and Neighbourhood Change." *Urban Studies* 41, no. 8 (2004): 1587–1600.

Cronyn, Joseph, and Evans Paull. "Heritage Tax Credits: Maryland's Own Stimulus to Renovate Buildings for Productive Use and Create Jobs, an $8.53 Return on Every State Dollar Invested." *Abell Report* 22, no. 1 (March 2009): 1–8.

Culhane, Dennis P., and Amy E. Hillier. "Comment on James R. Cohen's 'Abandoned Housing: Exploring Lessons from Baltimore.'" *Housing Policy Debate* 12, no. 3 (2001): 449–55.

Del Valle, Gaby. "Crown Heights Residents Protest Development at Bedford-Union Armory." *Gothamist*, March 8, 2017.

Ding, Lei, Jackelyn Hwang, and Eileen Divringi. "Gentrification and Residential Mobility in Philadelphia." *Regional Science and Urban Economics* 61 (2016): 38–51.

Duncan, Ian. "In 2010, Baltimore Had 16,800 Vacants. Eight Years and Millions of Dollars Later, the Number Is Down to 16,500." *Baltimore Sun,* February 27, 2018.

Ellen, Ingrid Gould, Keren Mertens Horn, and Davin Reed. *Has Falling Crime Invited Gentrification.* New York: NYU Furman Center, 2016.

Ellen, Ingrid Gould, Brian McCabe, and Eric Stern. *Fifty Years of Historic Preservation in New York City.* New York: NYU Furman Center, 2016.

Fein, David B. "Historic Districts: Preserving City Neighborhoods for the Privileged." *New York University Law Review* 60 (1985): 64.

Florida, Richard. *The Rise of the Creative Class.* New York: Basic, 2019.

Ford, Deborah Ann. "The Effect of Historic District Designation on Single-Family Home Prices." *Real Estate Economics* 17, no. 3 (1989): 353–62.

Freeman, Lance. "Displacement or Succession? Residential Mobility in Gentrifying Neighborhoods." *Urban Affairs Review* 40, no. 4 (2005): 463–91.

Freeman, Lance, and Frank Braconi. "Gentrification and Displacement New York City in the 1990s." *Journal of the American Planning Association* 70, no. 1 (2004): 39–52.

Gale, Dennis E. "The Impacts of Historic District Designation Planning and Policy Implications." *Journal of the American Planning Association* 57, no. 3 (1991): 325–40.

Galster, George, and Jason Booza. "The Rise of the Bipolar Neighborhood." *Journal of the American Planning Association* 73, no. 4 (2007): 421–35.

Gieryn, Thomas F. "What Buildings Do." *Theory and Society* 31, no. 1 (2002): 35–74.

Glaeser, Edward. "Preservation Follies: Excessive Landmarking Threatens to Make Manhattan a Refuge for the Rich." *City Journal* 20, no. 2 (2010).

——. *Triumph of the City: How Urban Spaces Make Us Human.* London: Pan Macmillan, 2011.

Goldwyn, Andrea Merrill. "Demolition by Neglect: A Loophole in Preservation Policy." Master's thesis, University of Pennsylvania, 1995.

Hackworth, Jason. "Demolition as Urban Policy in the American Rust Belt." *Environment and Planning A: Economy and Space* 48, no. 11 (2016): 2201–22.

——. "Race and the Production of Extreme Land Abandonment in the American Rust Belt." *International Journal of Urban and Regional Research* 42, no. 1 (2018): 51–73.

Hildebrandt, Rachel Ann. "Demolition-By-Neglect: Where Are We Now?" Master's thesis, University of Pennsylvania, 2012.

Holman, Nancy, and Gabriel M. Ahlfeldt. "No Escape? The Coordination Problem in Heritage Preservation." *Environment and Planning A: Economy and Space* 47, no. 1 (2015): 172–87.

Hubert, Craig. "Second Rental Building at Bedford-Union Armory Redevelopment Will Be Eight Stories With 60 Units." *Brownstoner*, June 15, 2018.

John, Matt. "Protestors Swarm Borough Hall to Oppose Bedford-Union Armory Development." *Brooklyn Paper*, July 13, 2017.

Kasinitz, Philip. "The Gentrification of 'Boerum Hill': Neighborhood Change and Conflicts Over Definitions." *Qualitative Sociology* 11, no. 3 (1988): 163–82.

Kidder, Jeffrey L. *Urban Flow: Bike Messengers and the City*. Ithaca, NY: Cornell University Press, 2012.

Klinenberg, Eric. *Heat Wave: A Social Autopsy of Disaster in Chicago*. Chicago: University of Chicago Press, 2015.

Knopp, Lawrence. "Some Theoretical Implications of Gay Involvement in an Urban Land Market." *Political Geography Quarterly* 9, no. 4 (1990): 337–52.

Lawrence, Denise L., and Setha M. Low. "The Built Environment and Spatial Form." *Annual Review of Anthropology* 19, no. 1 (1990): 453–505.

Lees, Loretta, Tom Slater, and Elvin Wyly. *Gentrification*. New York: Routledge, 2013.

Leichenko, Robin M., N. Edward Coulson, and David Listokin. "Historic Preservation and Residential Property Values: An Analysis of Texas Cities." *Urban Studies* 38, no. 11 (2001): 1973–87.

Lethem, Jonathan. *The Fortress of Solitude*. New York: Doubleday, 2003.

Levitt, Steven D. "Understanding Why Crime Fell in the 1990s: Four Factors That Explain the Decline and Six That Do Not." *Journal of Economic Perspectives* 18, no. 1 (2004): 163–90.

Listokin, David, Barbara Listokin, and Michael Lahr. "The Contributions of Historic Preservation to Housing and Economic Development." *Housing Policy Debate* 9, no. 3 (1998): 431–78.

Logan, Cameron. "Beyond a Boundary: Washington's Historic Districts and Their Racial Contents." *Urban History Review / Revue d'histoire Urbaine* 41, no. 1 (2012): 57–68.

Mallach, Alan. "Demolition and Preservation in Shrinking US Industrial Cities." *Building Research & Information* 39, no. 4 (2011): 380–94.

———. *What Drives Neighborhood Trajectories in Legacy Cities? Understanding the Dynamics of Change.* Cambridge, MA: Lincoln Institute of Land Policy, 2015.

Marcuse, Peter. "Gentrification, Abandonment, and Displacement: Connections, Causes, and Policy Responses in New York City." *Washington University Journal of Urban and Contemporary Law* 28 (1985): 195.

McCabe, Brian J., and Ingrid Gould Ellen. "Does Preservation Accelerate Neighborhood Change? Examining the Impact of Historic Preservation in New York City." *Journal of the American Planning Association* 82, no. 2 (2016): 134–46.

McKenzie, Evan. *Privatopia: Homeowner Associations and the Rise of Residential Private Government.* New Haven, CT: Yale University Press, 1994.

Mixson, Colin. "Armed with a New Backer: Crown Heights Pol Declares Newfound Support for City's Armory Scheme before Council." *Brooklyn Paper*, November 22, 2017.

———. "Pols: Show Us the Money! City Withholding Financial Details on Armory Deal, Lawmakers Say." *Brooklyn Paper*, August 16, 2017.

———. "Up in Arms: Legal Aid Lawyers Sue City Over Bedford-Union Armory Redevelopment Plan." *Brooklyn Paper*, December 4, 2017.

———. "Forward March: Builder Files Plans for New Tower at C'Heights Armory Amidst Ongoing Suit Against Project." *Brooklyn Paper*, June 20, 2018.

———. "No Aid: Judge Quashes Legal Aid Suit to Halt Bedford-Union Armory Development." *Brooklyn Paper*, July 30, 2018.

———. "Play Money: State Doles Out Millions to Fill Funding Gap for Promised Armory Rec Center." *Brooklyn Paper*, September 7, 2018.

Moloney, Brenna. *Putting the Right in Rightsizing.* Michigan Historic Preservation Network and National Trust for Historic Preservation, 2012.

Narwold, Andrew J. "Estimating the Value of the Historical Designation Externality." *International Journal of Housing Markets and Analysis* 1, no. 3 (2008): 288–95.

Narwold, Andrew, Jonathan Sandy, and Charles Tu. "Historic Designation and Residential Property Values." *International Real Estate Review* 11 (2008).

Newman, Galen, and Jesse Saginor. "Four Imperatives for Preventing Demolition by Neglect." *Journal of Urban Design* 19, no. 5 (2014): 622–37.

Newsom, Michael deHaven. "Blacks and Historic Preservation." *Law and Contemporary Problems* 36 (1971): 423.

Noonan, Douglas S. "Finding an Impact of Preservation Policies: Price Effects of Historic Landmarks on Attached Homes in Chicago, 1990–1999." *Economic Development Quarterly* 21, no. 1 (2007): 17–33.

Osman, Suleiman. *The Invention of Brownstone Brooklyn: Gentrification and the Search for Authenticity in Postwar New York*. New York: Oxford University Press, 2011.

Palen, J. John, and Bruce London. *Gentrification, Displacement, and Neighborhood Revitalization*. Albany, NY: SUNY Press, 1984.

Passell, Aaron. *Building the New Urbanism: Places, Professions, and Profits in the American Metropolitan Landscape*. New York: Routledge, 2013.

Pazmino, Gloria, and Sally Goldenberg. "Cumbo to Oppose Bedford Armory Project, After Hesitating for Months." *Politico PRO*, May 18, 2017.

Plitt, Amy. "Protestors Came Out En Masse at Meeting to Discuss Pfizer, Bedford-Union Armory Developments." *Curbed NY*, July 11, 2017.

Rickman, Dan S. "Neighborhood Historic Preservation Status and Housing Values in Oklahoma County, Oklahoma." *Journal of Regional Analysis and Policy* 39, no. 2 (2009): 1–10.

Rohn, Kacy. "Rebuilding Baltimore, from Urban Renewal to Project C.O.R.E.: Neighborhood Revitalization, Historic Preservation, and the Lessons of the Past." Master's thesis, University of Maryland, 2017.

Rosenberg, Zoe. "Bedford-Union Armory Redevelopment Hearing Postponed Amid Mounting Opposition." *Curbed NY*, January 1, 2017.

Ryberg-Webster, Stephanie. "Preserving Downtown America: Federal Rehabilitation Tax Credits and the Transformation of U.S. Cities." *Journal of the American Planning Association* 79, no. 4 (2013): 266–79.

——. "The Landscape of Urban Preservation: A Spatial Analysis of Federal Rehabilitation Tax Credits in Richmond, Virginia." *Journal of Urban Affairs* 37, no. 4 (2015): 410–35.

——. "Urban Policy in Disguise: A History of the Federal Historic Rehabilitation Tax Credit." *Journal of Planning History* 14, no. 3 (2015): 204–23.

Ryberg-Webster, Stephanie, and Kelly L. Kinahan. "Historic Preservation and Urban Revitalization in the Twenty-First Century." *Journal of Planning Literature* 29, no. 2 (2014): 119–39.

———. "Historic Preservation in Declining City Neighbourhoods: Analysing Rehabilitation Tax Credit Investments in Six US Cities." *Urban Studies* 54, no. 7 (2017): 1673–91.

Rypkema, Donovan. "The (Economic) Value of National Register Listing." *Cultural Resource Management* 1 (2002): 6–7.

———. *Historic Preservation and Affordable Housing: The Missed Connection.* National Trust for Historic Preservation, August 2002.

Rypkema, Donovan, Caroline Cheong, and Randall Mason. *Measuring Economic Impacts of Historic Preservation.* Advisory Council on Historic Preservation by PlaceEconomics, November 2011.

Sampson, Robert J. *Great American City: Chicago and the Enduring Neighborhood Effect.* Chicago: University of Chicago Press, 2012.

Sassen, Saskia. *The Global City: New York, London, Tokyo.* Princeton, NJ: Princeton University Press, 1991.

Schiszik, Lauren. "Equity in Historic Preservation Planning in Baltimore." Saving Places (blog), February 23, 2017, http://forum.savingplaces.org/blogs /special-contributor/2017/02/23/equity-in-historic-preservation-planning -in-baltimore.

Sharkey, Patrick. "The Intergenerational Transmission of Context." *American Journal of Sociology* 113, no. 4 (2008): 931–69.

Shaw, Kate. "Gentrification: What It Is, Why It Is, and What Can Be Done About It." *Geography Compass* 2, no. 5 (2008): 1697–1728.

Shaw, Kate S., and Iris W. Hagemans. " 'Gentrification Without Displacement' and the Consequent Loss of Place: The Effects of Class Transition on Low-Income Residents of Secure Housing in Gentrifying Areas.' " *International Journal of Urban and Regional Research* 39, no. 2 (2015): 323–41.

Sherman, Natalie. "New Program Aimed at Old Baltimore Vacants Problem Gets Slow Start." *Baltimore Sun,* September 24, 2016.

Smith, Neil. "Toward a Theory of Gentrification: A Back to the City Movement by Capital, Not People." *Journal of the American Planning Association* 45, no. 4 (1979): 538–48.

———. "Gentrification and Uneven Development." *Economic Geography* 58, no. 2 (1982): 139–55.

——. "Gentrification and the Rent Gap." *Annals of the Association of American Geographers* 77, no. 3 (1987): 462–65.

——. *The New Urban Frontier: Gentrification and the Revanchist City*. New York: Routledge, 2005.

Smith, Rachel Holliday. "Brooklyn Armory Deal, and Larger De Blasio Development Debate, Move Toward Term Two." *Gotham Gazette*, December 11, 2017.

Vigdor, Jacob L., Douglas S. Massey, and Alice M. Rivlin. "Does Gentrification Harm the Poor? [With Comments]." *Brookings-Wharton Papers on Urban Affairs* (2002): 133–82.

Walker, Ameena. "Bedford-Union Armory Redevelopment: News and Updates on the Brooklyn Project." *Curbed NY*, March 16, 2017.

——. "Crown Heights Residents Urge City to Nix Bedford-Union Armory Development Plans." *Curbed NY*, March 8, 2017.

Warerkar, Tanay. "Bedford-Union Armory Redevelopment Unanimously Rejected by Community Board." *Curbed NY*, June 28, 2017.

——. "Controversial Bedford-Union Armory Redevelopment Loses Cumbo's Support." *Curbed NY*, May 18, 2017.

——. "Embattled Bedford-Union Armory Conversion Clears City Planning Commission." *Curbed NY*, October 30, 2017.

——. "Embattled Bedford-Union Armory Project Is Endorsed by Mayor de Blasio." *Curbed NY*, September 13, 2017.

——. "Bedford-Union Armory in Crown Heights Gets New Renderings." *Curbed NY*, August 3, 2018.

——. "Bedford-Union Armory Revamp Moves Forward with Plans for 15-Story Rental." *Curbed NY*, March 14, 2018.

——. "Bedford-Union Armory's Community Center Gets $15M from Cuomo." *Curbed NY*, September 4, 2018.

Weiss, John M. "Protecting Landmarks from Demolition by Neglect: New York City's Experience." *Widener Law Review* 18 (2012): 309.

Wilson, David. "Making Historical Preservation in Chicago: Discourse and Spatiality in Neo-liberal Times." *Space and Polity* 8, no. 1 (2004): 43–59.

Zukin, Sharon, Scarlett Lindeman, and Laurie Hurson. "The Omnivore's Neighborhood? Online Restaurant Reviews, Race, and Gentrification." *Journal of Consumer Culture* 17, no. 3 (2017): 459–79.

INDEX

Page numbers in *italics* represent figures or tables.